THE CLERK OF BASINGSTOKE

THE CLERK OF BASINGSTOKE

A LIFE OF WALTER DE MERTON

by

MICHAEL FRANKS
Sometime Postmaster of Merton College

First published in 2003 by
Alden Press
Osney Mead
Oxford
OX2 0EF

British Library Cataloguing in Publication data

A catalogue record for this book is available from the British Library

ISBN 0-900040-33-5

Printed and bound in the UK by Alden Press, Oxford

CONTENTS

Preface

This book represents my debitum pietatis, a token of gratitude to Walter de Merton, whose endowment of Merton College enabled me to spend four years in Oxford as an undergraduate. At that time my knowledge of the Founder was somewhat hazy - not, I believe, an uncommon state of affairs.

My interest in Walter's life was aroused some years later on reading Dr. Roger Highfield's Early Rolls of Merton College and was quickened when I returned to live in North Hampshire in 1980 and discovered that Walter was the earliest of Basingstoke's (rather few) famous sons. I conceived the idea of a popular account of his life and achievements, which might be of interest both to members of Merton College and to those who live in parts of England with which Walter was connected in his long and distinguished career. I discussed my idea with Professor Geoffrey Martin at the War Years Gaudy in 1999. Slightly to my surprise Geoffrey was encouraging - professional historians are not always charitably inclined towards amateurs. A move to partial retirement in 2000 allowed me the time to start work.

Our knowledge of Walter's life is derived principally from patient research over a long period carried out by Merton scholars on the College archives and the public records, in particular by Bishop Hobhouse in the 19th.century, and in the 20th. by Professor H.W. Garrod, Dr. Roger Highfield and Professor Geoffrey Martin. This book draws extensively on the work of those who have gone before in pursuit of my objective - to produce, in a single accessible volume, a narrative which is accurate, readable and attractively presented.

The preparation of a popular Life has also brought to light some new material - for example as regards Walter's character and personal appearance; his personal manor of Basingstoke Merton (sometimes Watermartens), and the place and circumstances of his death in 1277. Being able to offer these modest contributions to academic scholarship is an added bonus.

Writing this book has taken me into wholly unfamiliar territory but I have found the task both interesting and enjoyable. If its readers are able to share some part of this interest and pleasure the effort will have been well worthwhile.

All profits from the book will go to the Development Fund of Merton College.

Sources and Acknowledgments

The main published sources for Walter's life are Bishop Hobhouse's Sketch of the Life of Walter de Merton, published in 1859, Dr. Roger Highfield's The Early Rolls of Merton College (1964), the early chapters of A History of Merton College by Professor Geoffrey Martin and Dr. Roger Highfield (1997) and the article "Walter de Merton" in the Dictionary of National Biography (soon to be replaced by a new article written by Professor Martin)

Walter figures frequently in the English public records and in numerous documents relating to land transactions, many of which are reproduced in The History of Basingstoke by F.J. Baigent & J.E. Millard (1889) "a most valuable contribution to the history of Hampshire". Other published sources are listed on page 119, and all sources are recorded in the Notes to the text.

In writing this book I have received generous and valuable help from Professor Geoffrey Martin (who encouraged me to start) and Dr. Roger Highfield, Emeritus Fellow of Merton College. Both have read the text, eliminated errors and made many positive suggestions. However any mistakes and misjudgments which remain are my own.

On a number of specific topics I have had generous assistance from Mr. Thomas Braun, Dean of Merton College and Dr. Sarah Bendall, Librarian and Archivist of Merton College (until September 2000 when she returned to Emmanuel College, Cambridge). Mr. Braun produced virtually overnight the elegant English translation of the obituary verses on Walter by the Osney Abbey Chronicler (see Appendix II) and of the inscription placed on Walter's tomb in 1598.

I would like to acknowledge with thanks the help which I have had from Mr. Ernie Major of the Willis Museum, Basingstoke; Mrs. Anne Hawker of Basingstoke, particularly on her research into the manor of Basingstoke Merton (sometimes Watermartens); Miss Barbara Webb of Worcester Park, who guided me round Walter's manor of Malden, straddling the Hogsmill River; Mr. David Rymill and his colleagues at the Hampshire Record Office; Mr. Brett Dolman of the British Library; Dr. Tony Trowles, Librarian of Westminster Abbey, and the office of the Dean of Rochester.

On illustrations and maps, I must first thank Mr. Alan Bott, Bodley Fellow of Merton College, who generously made available photographs and a map from his personal collection of Merton College images. I acknowledge with thanks the permission to reproduce images given by the Bodleian Library (the portrait by Sonmans of Walter); the British Library (four scenes from the Luttrell Psalter and the image of Walter's seal as Bishop of Rochester); English Heritage (the aerial photograph of Rievault Abbey); Mrs. Anne Hawker (Map of the Basingstoke Open Fields); the Museum of London Archaeology Service (plan of Merton Priory in relation to the modern roads); Phillimore & Co. Ltd (Mediaeval Trading Map of Hampshire, from A History of Hampshire by B.A. Turner 1978); The National Library of Scotland (Plan of Basingstoke) and Mr. Philip Shewan (Extracts from maps of Surrey and North Hampshire by J & G Cary 1822)

I am indebted to Ashley Briggs who took numerous photographs and provided the graphic design for the book and its cover.

Finally, I must acknowledge with thanks the generosity of Mr. William Alden. He proposed that the Alden Press should act as publisher as well as printer and, with his colleague Mr. Andrew Hopwood, provided extensive advice and support throughout.

Introduction

Visiting 13th.century England as a non-historian is like travelling to a foreign country - perhaps some remote corner of Europe (or some rural area of England in the early 20th. Century). The physical features are hardly different, though there are not the tidy fields and hedges which we are used to in many parts of modern England. There are no motorways or railways, of course, but the main and minor roads and the towns and villages are where we expect to see them.

The place names are much the same (though the spelling might have changed) so that rivers, hills, lakes, marshy ground, even fields can be identified, in addition to the roads and streets in the towns

Except in the wild places there is much agricultural activity, involving lots of people, assisted by horses and oxen. Every river and stream supports water mills

Ploughing

A Post Windmill

along its length and there are windmills on high ground. Superficially, it all looks quite familiar.

But there are of course many differences. While in a physical sense mediaeval England is recognisable, the structure of the kingdom and of society is quite different. The King, as the descendant of the Conqueror, is the centre of almost everything but while he has overriding authority he has to rule with the broad support of his magnates - and he has to cooperate with the Church. The Papal Legate is a power in the land.

A Watermill

The King and the magnates are constantly moving through their domains, combining their public duties with management of their privately owned estates and indulging their leisure amusements, particularly hunting. Their servants, similarly, are always on the move, either following their masters or managing their masters' affairs - land, castles, religious houses, churches, buildings, forests and so on.

Altogether there is much more travelling than one might expect, and many quite humble folk go on pilgrimage when to-day they might take a package holiday. England was surprisingly cosmopolitan, with constant exchange with the English domains in France, and many "foreigners" at all levels of society. The Church, of course, was entirely international, and churchmen were regularly transferred between English and European positions. Knowledge of overseas countries was spread by international traders and merchant seamen. An important factor was the universality of Latin as the language of the Church, international diplomacy and scholarship.

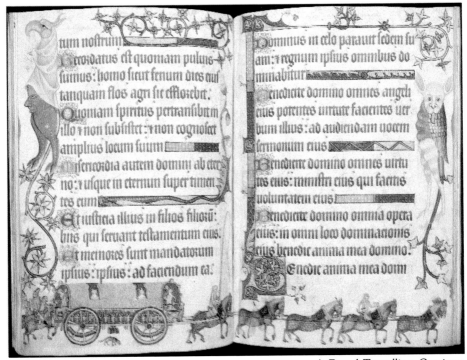

A Royal Travelling Carriage

English society was structured, inclusive and cohesive: everyone was involved in interlocking personal relationships covering most aspects of life - working the land or following a trade, buying and selling foodstuffs and all other retail products and services, maintaining public order, in attending "courts" for both legal and administrative purposes. And those in the upper and middle ranks of society all participated too, observing their duties to the King and their feudal superiors and taking an active role in local government and the administration of justice.

While society was tightly structured it was at the same time "open" - in that men of ability and energy could, and frequently did, rise from obscurity to prominence and wealth in Church and State. Military prowess and commercial skill, as always, provided means of advancement, but the single most important key was education, organised by or under the supervision of the Church. Promotion by merit was implicit in the system - the King and the magnates of Church and State needed men of ability to organise their armies, conduct their diplomacy, run national and local government and manage their possessions, which were mainly land related. There was no organised system of recruitment so young men of promise were sought out by "talent-spotting" and "networking".

The subject of this book, Walter de Merton, was one of the outstanding examples of preferment by merit in 13th. Century England. He stood head and shoulders above almost all his contemporaries in ability, character, physical stature - and wealth.

Walter's surname "de Merton" itself reflects his rise in life, being derived from his association from boyhood with the Augustinian Merton Priory. Merton is in Surrey, some 7 miles south west from Westminster, and over 40 miles from Walter's home territory, Basingstoke, further south west, in Hampshire. Walter and his kin were very much a Hampshire family. We have no proof that he was born in Basingstoke but it seems probable as his parents lived there and owned property in and around the town.

As will appear, there is limited factual evidence about much of Walter's personal life, and what there is has been patiently discovered or deduced over a long period by scholars working mainly on the archives of Merton College, Oxford and the English public records. While this lack of evidence is obviously frustrating it is not critical for present purposes since Walter's main claim to our attention and interest rests upon his achievements during his life and his educational legacy – which are well recorded.

The lack of detail, too, does not prevent us from recognising a fascinating, multi-faceted character, at ease in all levels of society, a clerk who (eventually) became a bishop; a much loved and respected counsellor and friend; a generous host; a senior Royal servant (King's Clerk); Chancellor of England (twice, and effectively Regent when Edward I was away on Crusade); a successful property speculator and developer; a first class lawyer and conveyancer; an educational visionary, and – at all times a devoted "family man".

Origins

(There is an outline family tree in Appendix I)

It is generally agreed that Walter was born between 1195 and 1210. Since there is no more exact knowledge we will assume, in the interests of simplicity, that he was born in 1200 so that his age will march in step with the years of the 13th.century. His birthplace was probably Basingstoke, a prosperous market town in north east Hampshire which (together with the "hundred" of Basingstoke i.e. a wide area around the town) was part of the royal demesne, that is, directly held by the Crown without the involvement of a magnate or royal "tenant-in-chief" - which was the normal situation in England following the Conquest in 1066.

The name Walter seems to have come from his paternal grandfather. Walter's father was named William, sometimes known as Cook ("Le Cuk"). While resident in Basingstoke, William, or his forebears, appears to have come originally from Herriard, a village 4 miles to the south east of Basingstoke.

William was a cousin to Richard de Herriard, a Royal judge in the reigns of Richard I and John; and therefore perhaps also related to Edmond de Herriard who became prior of Merton Priory in 1296. By a coincidence this same Richard de Herriard, with two other senior public servants, was charged in 1195-6 with assessing the tallage - the liability to municipal tax - of the demesnes of Basingstoke. [2] The Herriard family were major benefactors of the Nunnery of Hartley Wintney (8 miles north east of Basingstoke) - Sir Richard Herriard senior built the first stone church at Hartley Wintney – and four members of the family were commemorated in the convent calendar. [3] A number of Herriards (there are many variations of the name) lived and held property in Basingstoke in the 13th.century, and they were no doubt related to Walter through his father. [4] Walter's legacy to "the Nuns of Wyntneye" in his will may echo his relationship to the Herriard family.

overleaf; North East Hampshire

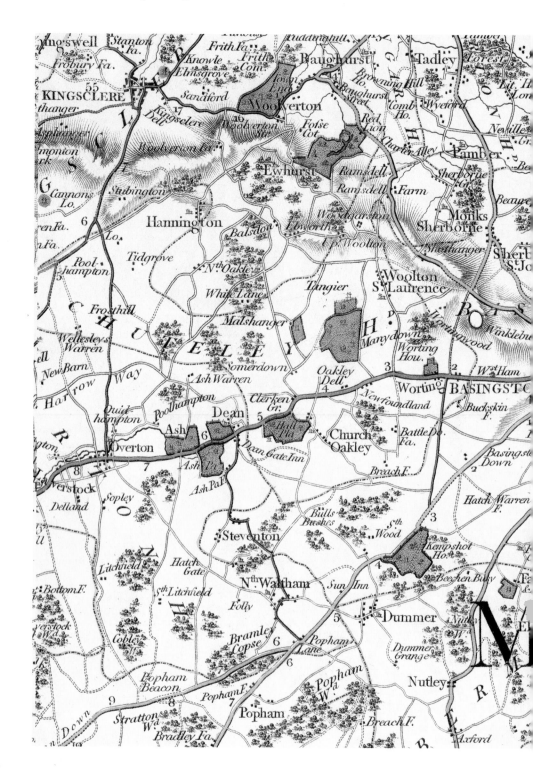

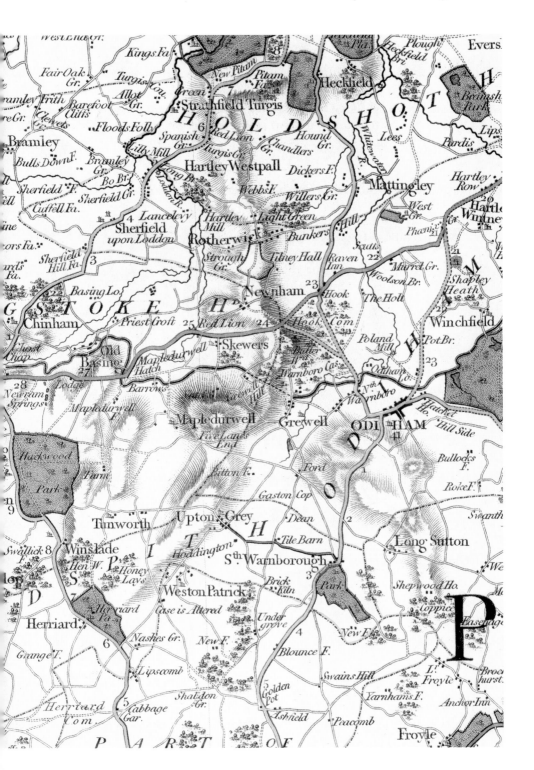

William and his family would to-day be described as "yeoman" or "middle class" and, as we shall see, the same applied to Walter's mother, about whom a little more is known. Despite his name, William was not a cook by occupation: Cook was a well-known local name and a number of Cooks appear throughout Walter's life, for example in his "household" when he became important, and some of them may have been his kinsmen.[5] It is not known whether William owned land on his own account but he appears to have had a life interest in the main Basingstoke property where the family lived.

Walter's mother was Christina FitzOliver (sometimes FitzAce, probably her mother's family, as she had an uncle John FitzAce). The FitzOlivers were a well-established, prominent Basingstoke family, and Christina, through her family, owned freehold property in the town and in the surrounding "open fields"; which made her a direct tenant of the King.

While earlier there had been only two such "fields" by the thirteenth century there were three, and possibly four - Northfield (later Holy Ghost), Middlefield, Westfield (later Salisbury) and S o u t h f i e l d (Winchester). The Open Fields were sown with arable crops, though they were also grazed after harvest and during their fallow period. The area of fields increased over time, as more land was cleared and ploughed, and the number of fields increased too, though this probably was in part as a result of sub-division.

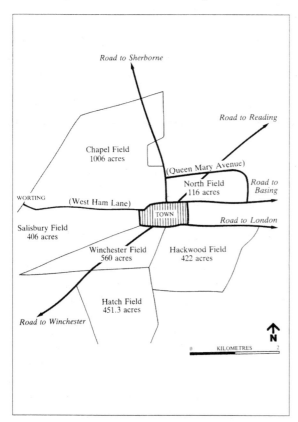

The Basingstoke Open Fields

There was also common land to the east of

Basingstoke and the "down" ("Down Grange House" still survives) to the southwest where the right to run stock was based on the arable acreage held in the "fields". The community appointed a swineherd and and a hayward (cattle keeper) to act for everyone, while the sheep were combined into three or more flocks, and there were detailed rules governing the cooperative farming system, which was overseen by the Court of the Hundred and the Manorial Court Leet. [6] (Under the special arrangements between the King and the town the men of Basingstoke were effectively the Lord of the Manor). There were also privately owned meadows, pastures, marshes, fisheries, orchards and gardens in and near the town.

The area of the open fields increased over time to more than 3000 acres and the Down was around a further 600. The open field system continued until the introduction of enclosures in the late 18th.century, but from around 1300 onwards there was a gradual consolidation of ownership into fewer hands.

Christina had a sister Margaret (Walter's aunt) who married a William Chastayne de Kyngsmylle, and produced nine children. They appear (through the connection with the King's Mill at Basingstoke from which they took their name - one of the three mills in the town) to be the original source of the well-known English (and Irish) Kingsmill family. Christina also had a brother Robert FitzOliver who had at least four children. Walter thus had some 13 cousins who with their descendants, in due course, became beneficiaries of his family devotion, together with his siblings - seven sisters - and their descendants, to whom we now turn.

Walter had seven sisters and no brothers. Walter is assumed to be the oldest child. All seven sisters married and produced children. One, Edith, married twice. Of the eight husbands, five, (to judge by their last names which are recognisable place names) were Hampshire men. Of the other three, one came from Wiltshire (Wylye), one from Surrey (Ewell, probably introduced to his sister Agnes by Walter when he obtained his first Church living in Surrey) and one (the second husband of Edith) from Buckinghamshire. Walter appears to have arranged property settlements for four of his sisters on or soon after the marriages (Alice, Agnes, Castania and Edith) and to have transferred substantial properties later in his life to benefit the families of Castania (again) and Cristina.[7] This seems to have been altogether out of his own resources.

In due course, too, Walter provided for all the nephews and nieces, and their descendants. These benefits took at least four forms - educational opportunities at Merton College which Walter founded and endowed; employment in his "household" when he rose in the royal service; ecclesiastical preferment; and, on his death, legacies under his will and succession to real property which he still owned.

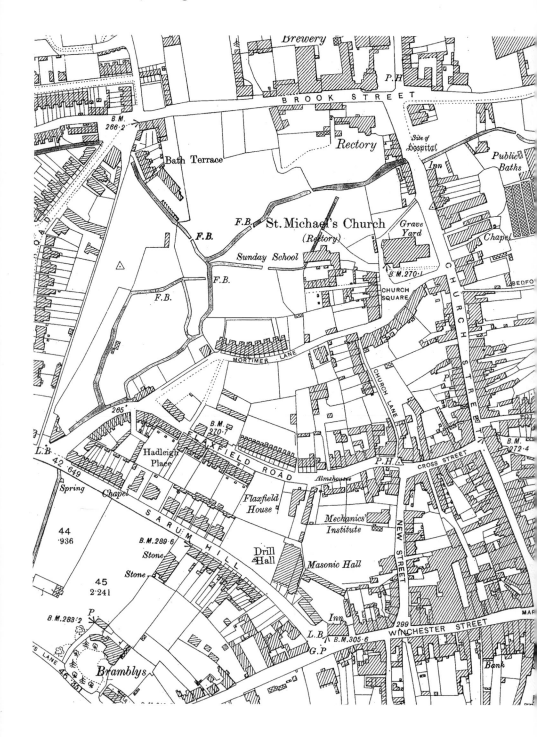

Central Basingstoke

The scale of Walter's practical support for his family can be fully appreciated only if it is borne in mind that this support was in addition to the substantial endowments which Walter provided for the Hospital of St.John the Baptist (a charitable house in Basingstoke for travellers and for the poor, sick, and elderly) from around 1239 and for Merton College (which Walter founded as a new type of institution for higher education) from around 1262. Walter's endowment of the Basingstoke Hospital came mainly from the family property which he inherited, but all the other family and charitable gifts (amounting to many millions of pounds in 2000 money: see chapter 11) were organised and paid for out of his own resources by a man who worked at high pressure throughout his life for the Church and the Crown.

Walter, his sisters and parents lived in the middle of Basingstoke on the north bank of the River Loddon, but with some land also on the south side of the River. Their home was close to the church of St.Michael (the predecessor of the present fifteenth century church, which incorporates some parts of the earlier building) - the situation underlines the family's standing in the town. At some later date, Walter appears to have had a house of his own next to his parents'. No trace remains, at least above ground, of the buildings but it seems probable that Walter transferred this central property, around 1240, after the death of his parents and the marriage of all his sisters, to accommodate the Hospital of St.John the Baptist. His mother died first, and there are two undated transfers of

St.Michael's, Basingstoke: St.Stephen's Chapel, in the left foreground, was the structure known to Walter and his parents

land to the Hospital (apparently executed with only a short interval between them) suggesting that the second followed on his father's death. (Both parents were buried in St.Michael's Church, Basingstoke, possibly in St.Stephen's Chapel)

If, as seems to be the case, it was the family property (perhaps with Walter's own house added) that was transferred to the Hospital, the site can be precisely identified, since the main streets of Basingstoke remained unchanged from the Middle Ages - until the new "Town Centre" was built in the 1960s.

Merton Farmhouse

After the Hospital declined it was eventually replaced by a building called Merton Farmhouse (built in 1778), which stood south east of the intersection between Church Street and Brook Street (sometimes "Northbrook Street"). The property was known as Merton Farm and (in the nineteenth century) it stretched along Brook Street on the north side of the River Loddon as far as the Barge Inn in Wote Street. According to Merton College records the property was sold to the tenant Henry Portsmouth in 1887 [8] (He was Mayor of Basingstoke in 1875-6), and the Hospital buildings were demolished in the same year. By the end of the 19th.century Merton Farmhouse was occupied by Edmund Portsmouth (who had been miller of the Eastrop Mill) and, included, apart from the house "a large barn, stables and sheds and stretched along Brook Street as far as the old Fire Station".[9] The River Loddon ran at the bottom of the garden and Mr.Portsmouth "had a rustic bridge with an archway of roses leading to a summerhouse where he used to have smoking parties".[10] His southern boundary was the Self Defence Inn.

The farmhouse was in turn demolished at the end of the nineteenth century and on the site of the house, the gardens and the farmyard was built in 1901 a new St.John's School, established by Dr.Cooper Smith, the vicar of Basingstoke.[11] The River Loddon was piped underneath the playground. The school building was, in its turn, demolished in the 1960s to accommodate the new "Town Centre" shopping mall. The 18th.century Basingstoke vicarage (now known as Chute

Looking south up Church Street. On the right the Old Rectory. Merton Farmhouse stood opposite on the left.

House) still stands south west of the old intersection between Church Street and Brook Street i.e.opposite the site of Merton Farmhouse, although the rector is to-day accommodated in a smaller, modern vicarage.

The new shopping mall, combined with the absorption of "London overspill" population, and the closure of a livestock market, which had flourished for 150 years (replacing the stock market originally held in the Market Place at the top of Church Street and Wote Street) ended Basingstoke's long career as an agricultural market town. St. John's School moved to another site in the town.

The site on which stood successively Walter's family home, the Hospital of St.John and St.John's School is now under the service area of the shopping mall, still straddling the River Loddon in its underground culvert. At the southern end of the site is The Bass Public House and Ladbrokes' betting shop built high above the ground over the service area of the shopping mall. The pub is probably the lineal descendant of the Self Defence Inn, which stood in roughly the same position, and formed the southern boundary of the Merton Farmhouse plot.

We have no direct evidence of William Cook's occupation. Given the family ownership of a sizeable area of land in the "fields", probably some 60 acres, the fact that Basingstoke was a farming community, and no suggestion of a trade, he was probably a working farmer, though it is likely that the family also received rent and/or services from agricultural tenants.

Biology and Morphology

Basing and Basingstoke

Some comments on the relationship between these two communities may be useful, first, to dispel the confusion that tends to arise and, secondly, because Basing and its surrounding area provide some clues as to Walter's choice of career.

Basing (even now often referred to as "Old Basing") lies 2 miles to the north east of Basingstoke. At some time prior to the Conquest "Basing" appears to have described the whole area, but by the time of the Domesday Book (1086) there were two distinct communities, Basing and Basingstoke. "Stoke" or "stoc" implies a dependent settlement, but even by the Conquest Basingstoke had overtaken Basing.

Basingstoke was recorded in the Domesday Book as held by King William in demesne (that is, in his own hands), having a church and a market, with 20 villeins, 8 bordars with 12 plough teams, 6 serfs and 12 freemen, and 3 mills. Basing was somewhat smaller: it measured 6 1/2 hides and was held by Hugh de Port with 7 serfs and 3 mills. It seems clear that, even by 1086, the Basingstoke offshoot had outstripped the original or parent community, and this process continued. As part of the royal demesne Basingstoke developed a measure of municipal self government at an early stage.[1] In 1203 the market day was changed from Sunday to Monday, and again in 1214 to Wednesday. At that time the town was about the same size as Alton: Winchester was twice its size and Southampton four times as large - this can be deduced from an order of King John in 1212 demanding the provision of armed men from these four Hampshire towns.[2]

Prosperous "market towns" and "county towns" have often developed from communities which in earlier times formed part of the royal demesne, probably because of the absence of a feudal lord who, in person or through his officials, tended to dominate the community and perhaps inhibit its entrepreneurial ambitions.[3] The growth of Basingstoke, compared to its near neighbour Basing (under the shadow of the de Port's castle), seems to be a good example.

Mediaeval Hampshire - Trading Patterns

Basingstoke continued to prosper as an agricultural market town and as a pro-
ducer of woollen cloth from the local sheep[4], and as an important staging post
in the English transport system on the main routes between London and
Southampton and London and Salisbury and the South West. In the heyday of
the coaching system over 50 coaches called at Basingstoke every day. At the end
of the eighteenth century the Basingstoke canal was completed, linking the town
via the River Wey to the Thames, and in the nineteenth and twentieth centuries
Basingstoke became a busy railway junction.[5] Arable farming supported a
major malting activity in Basingstoke, and the efficient communications
attracted manufacturing industry in the nineteenth century.

After the Conquest in 1066 Basing was granted by King William to Hugh de Port, and it became the chief of his 55 lordships in Hampshire. Like many Norman magnates he built a castle on his estate at Basing; in this case an unusually large motte and bailey, the remains of which can still be seen. It gradually decayed and on its site the Paulet family, who had inherited it, built the fortified mansion known as Basing House in the sixteenth century

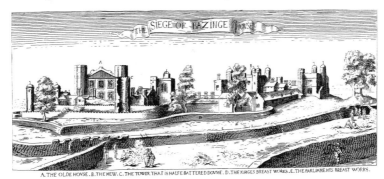

Basing House by Hollar

Basing House was besieged and eventually taken by the Cromwellian forces in the Civil War. By order of the House of Commons - on the Protector's recommendation - Basing House was to be "totally slighted and demolished" and the local inhabitants were encouraged to assist - "whoever fetches away the materials shall have them for their pains": some can be seen to this day built into the Old Basing houses.[6]

In the twelfth century the Basing parish church of St.Mary (the predecessor of the present church built in the sixteenth century) was the "mother" church of St.Michael's Basingstoke, no doubt reflecting the original pre-Conquest pre-eminence of Basing described above.[7] In 1233 the Bishop of Winchester Peter des Roches purchased the advowsons of the churches of Basing and Basingstoke (that is, the right to appoint the priests) from the Abbot and Convent of Mont St.Michel (to whom they had been given by William the Conqueror) and in 1234 granted them to a newly established Priory at Selborne in Hampshire. The arrangements for services in the two churches made following this change (in 1244) stationed the vicar in Basingstoke and two chaplains in Basing, thus starting the process of demoting Basing to a dependent chapelry: Basing became a separate parish only in 1864.[8] These arrangements no doubt reflected the size and prosperity of the two communities. The advowsons of Basing and Basingstoke passed at the Dissolution to Magdalen College, Oxford where they have remained.

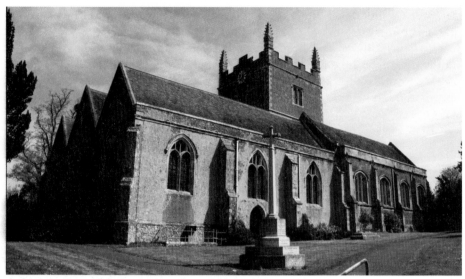

St.Mary's, Basing: little remains from before the 15th.century

The Rector of Basing from 1204 until after 1231 was one Philip de Lucy, a kinsman of Godfrey de Lucy, Bishop of Winchester 1180-1206. He was at the same time vicar of Cuddington in Surrey (from 1205 until his death in about 1233) and also Rector of Selborne (from about 1197).

The parish of Cuddington was in the gift of Merton Priory. After Philip de Lucy's death (around 1233) Merton Priory appointed Walter to the living: he was then about 33. At the time of Walter's appointment to Cuddington the Prior of Merton was Henry de Basinges, elected just two years before. From his name it is likely that he came from Basing. Another Basing man was connected to Merton Priory a little earlier. A deed around 1180 executed by the Priory in favour of a retired employee was witnessed by a Master Geoffrey de Basing.[9]

Another locally bred churchman and scholar, particularly skilled in Greek, was John of Basing (or Basingstoke). He is thought to have studied in Oxford, Paris and Athens and was Archdeacon of Leicester by 1235. He was a friend of the famous scholar and churchman Grosseteste (who figured in Walter's life a little later, as we shall see). John died in 1252, so he was roughly contemporary with Walter and may well have known him. Certainly, if (as seems to be the case) he originated in Basing or Basingstoke, his family would have been known to Walter's parents.

The three men with Merton Priory connections - Geoffrey de Basing, Henry de

Basinges and Philip de Lucy - must have been known to Walter's family in Basingstoke and Geoffrey and Henry may have been related to them.

The personal connections between Merton Priory and North Hampshire may have been coincidental or they may have resulted from a deliberate practice of recruiting from areas in which the Priory had property interests (like the policy adopted by Merton College - see chapter 8 - of recruiting undergraduates from areas where the College has investments).

Merton Priory in the early 13th. century also had several property links with the Basing/Basingstoke district.[10]

In Basing and Basingstoke themselves there is no hard evidence of the Priory holding land at that period. In around 1236 Walter (by then established as a clerk at Merton Priory) acted as attorney to Henry de Basinges, the Prior of Merton, in an action concerning land at Basingstoke[11]; and in the 14th.and 15th.centuries the Priory paid rent for a property in Basingstoke called Vine House, alias Wynbow's[12]: these or other properties may have been owned by the Priory at an earlier date. There is a further, intriguing connection: in the 1274 Inquisition ordered by Edward I into the Royal interests in Basingstoke a complaint was made that the Prior of Merton had unjustly erected a gallows within the hundred of Basingstoke. The Inquisition looked back to the previous reign of Henry III though we have no way of fixing the date: the allegation reflects an assertion of lordship based on land holding.

Some 5 miles north east of Basing Merton Priory held the important manor of Holdshott (sometimes "Holdshot" or "Putham").[13] Holdshott was the name of the most northerly of the Basingstoke "outer" hundreds. The nucleus of the manor appears to have been a grant to the Priory in around 1208 by John de Port, grandson of the magnate Hugh de Port mentioned above, of one hide of land in Heckfield (perhaps some 100 acres), a wood, a meadow and common rights of pasture. About the same time the Priory acquired land in the neighbouring parish of Mattingley from the Oakley family; a hide of land in Putham; and a wood in Hazeley from King John. There was also land held by the Priory from the twelfth century in the next-door parish of Hartley Wespall. These other parcels all became part of the manor of Holdshott. The priory established a non-parochial chapel in their manor, and there were agreements concerning the apportionment of tithes with the incumbents of Hartley and Heckfield parishes. Holdshott was an important holding of the Priory, retained until the Dissolution.

In 1222 Merton Priory acquired the advowson of Sherfield on Loddon, some 3 miles north of Basing.[14]. In around 1236 the Priory acquired land at Upton Grey (Upton), 5 miles south east of Basingstoke.[15]

Early Life and Education

We have virtually no direct evidence of this period of Walter's life. The tradition and probability is that he was educated either at Merton Priory in Surrey, or elsewhere at the Priory's expense. He may also have studied in Oxford, residing at Mauger Hall. There are suggestions, too, that at some time Walter studied, and possibly later practised, law in London.

It has been established that there was a flourishing school for boys at Merton Priory in the twelfth century (Thomas Becket was educated there) but it is not certain that it was still operating in the early years of the 13th; though the Priory certainly at that time was giving financial assistance to promising young men associated with it to study elsewhere.[1] The tradition is perfectly reasonable, so we may adopt it, and - as we will see - there is some circumstantial evidence supporting a period of study at Oxford University.

We may therefore assume that Walter was sent to school at Merton Priory at around 8 years old and that he followed what we would now call "the national curriculum" - in the Middle Ages the Church organised or supervised all schools - written and spoken Latin, followed by "Grammar", namely syntax, Latin literature, rhetoric and logical disputation. Whether he went on to arithmetic, geometry and astronomy we do not know. We may speculate that he was also trained in music and singing, and various social skills, for example, acting as a page, taking part in presentations and entertainments, and receiving guests visiting the Priory.

In the thirteenth century students went to university at an early age - sometimes as young as 12 or 13. The view of scholars is that Walter, if he went to Oxford (as we are assuming), did not complete what we would now call a full degree course.[2] Because of this, and the period of unrest at Oxford (described below) which was not finally settled until 1214, it seems likely that he went to Oxford at a somewhat later age, perhaps for a period between his 15th. and 20th. years. We may speculate that at Oxford he studied theology and law, and it seems quite likely (as we will discuss below) that he was a pupil of the famous Oxford scholar Adam de Marisco (Marsh). As we will see, too, it is possible that he lodged at Mauger Hall in the Cornmarket.

Based on the legal skills which he displayed in later life, it seems reasonable to deduce that Walter, at some stage, received some formal education in law. At Oxford civil i.e.Roman, law and canon (ecclesiastical) law were both taught. The English common i.e, customary law, was not, so far as we know - although Professor F.W.Maitland speculated that it may have been.[3] Training in the common law was obtainable mainly in London - both Westminster and the City - but also in other towns where royal and local courts were held.[4] Such training was organised by apprenticeship to established practitioners. The most important part of the common law in the thirteenth century was land law and conveyancing - the preparation of documents dealing mainly with land and the many rights and duties related to it, but also other matters e.g. wills, manumission of villeins, commercial contracts, loans of money.[5] This part of legal practice *outside the Courts* was also carried on *by practitioners having no formal qualification* in the central government offices, in the households of large landowners and in religious houses; so legal training was available there too, again on an apprenticeship or "understudying" basis.[6] (Professor Maitland has analysed a precedent book containing over 40 commonly used documents prepared in the 1270s by a monk in Luffield Priory, in Buckinghamshire, including a letter from a student to his father seeking more funds: we may assume that the student was at Oxford). We must also note that, for a working lawyer in the service of the King, a magnate or a religious house the civil, canon and common laws were not mutually exclusive. For example, Church rights might be governed either by canon or common law. Wills and matrimonial matters were governed by canon law. Bonds - the formal undertaking to pay money - could be subject to all three legal systems. So any useful, practical lawyer needed knowledge of all three.[7]

In the middle of the thirteenth century the royal judges were not yet appointed exclusively from the ranks of practising lawyers - many were "generalist" public servants - so that in developing the English common law the Courts were often using principles drawn from civil and canon law.

If Walter had never moved beyond Merton Priory it would probably have been possible for him to pick up sufficient law from one or more of the "in house" practitioners. Since he was recruited to the royal service - presumably on his performance to date and his potential for the wider challenge of royal service - and in the light of his subsequent distinguished performance as Judge in the Palatinate Court and as Bishop's Chancellor at Durham, as a King's Clerk, in international advocacy and negotiation, as a judge in the Jewish exchequer court &c. it seems likely that he also studied law elsewhere, probably both at Oxford and in London. On that basis we might assign some legal study in London, perhaps followed by some practice of the law, to a period between his 18th. and 25th. years.

In support of the case for Walter's time in London as an apprentice, and perhaps also as a practising, lawyer, there is usually quoted a deed dated to around 1240 in which Robert de Wautham quit claimed Walter for land acquired at Basingstoke (previously owned by Robert's father) for 40 shillings cash and a promise by Walter to find Robert some office or employment in London or elsewhere within 12 months.[8]

Whatever the exact nature, and timing, of his legal training we may assume that by his early 20s Walter was back at Merton priory as a "trainee clerk". It seems likely that the practical work of managing the affairs of an organisation like the Priory was also taught on an "apprenticeship" basis i.e. learning by understudying more senior and experienced colleagues. This would extend to land management and agriculture (including visiting and inspection of Priory estates), drafting letters and formal documents, accounting, auditing, record-keeping, conducting negotiations, representing the Priory in court, making presentations, advising the Prior and the like.

It may be worth noting at this point that in the thirteenth century working "full-time" did not prevent personal entrepreneurial activity for private account. It was, if anything, encouraged. In the same way good work and loyal service were often rewarded by granting sinecures (more easily available to grateful employers than ready cash), and, in addition, holders of public offices were entitled to exact fees from members of the public quite separately from the stipend of their office. In this way successful public servants could quickly accumulate very considerable personal wealth. Ironically, in modern times public servants in England receive only their stipend and an inflation-proofed pension (though they may, on retirement, join the ranks of "the good and the great" and look for further rewards). The rapid accumulation of private wealth to-day is restricted to entertainers, entrepreneurs and directors of joint stock enterprises. Does this difference influence the choice of career of promising young people to-day? Walter received his first church preferment (the parish of Cuddington in Surrey) at around the age of 33, and many others followed.

Before taking an overview of Merton Priory and Oxford at this time - early in the thirteenth century - there are two interesting preliminary questions to be considered. First, why did a well-to-do Hampshire family with land to farm (and probably a property portfolio to manage), with a number of daughters (eventually seven) to settle in life, launch their only son into a career in the Church, rather than training him up to develop the family's prosperity and continue the family line ? We cannot answer this question directly but we can speculate that the Church was, as ever, "talent-spotting" and identified Walter at an early age. He was, we know, in adult life tall and well built and in addition exceptionally intelligent and energetic, as well as being charming and popular, and these attributes may have shown themselves in the boy. Whoever wished to extend patronage to Walter - perhaps it was Henry de Basinges, who subsequently became Prior of Merton - must have convinced Walter's parents that the education and career prospects which Merton Priory could offer would be of greater benefit both to Walter and the family. At that stage no one could know that Walter would eventually gain royal patronage, so the idea must have been sold to his parents on the basis of a successful career in the Church.

Secondly, why Merton Priory? As indicated above, there were certainly connections between the Priory and the Basing/Basingstoke area, through property ownership, through identified individuals and a practice - perhaps even a policy - of recruiting in the North Hampshire area (Basingstoke is nearly 40 miles from Merton).[9] Walter's parents would have known Geoffrey de Basing, Philip de Lucy, the rector of Basing and Henry de Basinges, (a brother and later sub-cellarer and Prior of the Priory), and there may have been some kinship.

Since Walter's course in life was decided before he reached his teens, he himself could have had little say in the decision. Finding himself destined to a celibate, childless career in the Church may go some way to explaining the quite extraordinary devotion which he displayed throughout his long life (and through his will), to his parents and their memory, to his sisters and their husbands and issue, and furthermore to his many cousins, together with their spouses and descendants.

Merton Priory

By any standards - spiritual, educational, financial, political - Merton Priory was in the early thirteenth century a true "power-house". It had been founded 100 years before by Henry I in about 1117 on land provided near the River Wandle by Gilbert the Norman who was sheriff of Surrey.

He invited the Augustinian Canons - one of the most dynamic missionary orders at the time - to settle there. A rapid building programme was undertaken on its 60 acres which produced six chapels, a guest house, an infirmary, a large cloister, the priory church and the chapter house. The size and lay-out was similar to that of the Cistercian Rievaulx Abbey in Yorkshire.

Rievaulx Abbey

The new foundation enjoyed Royal support from the start: Queen Matilda visited in 1118 with Prince William, who was tragically drowned two years later in the White Ship disaster. The Priory had close relations with Richard I, John and Henry III, particularly the last-named, who showered gifts on the house, visited it frequently and maintained special accommodation there, both for himself and for the conduct of state business e.g the Statute of Merton was promulgated there in 1236. Thomas Becket studied at Merton and also, according to tradition, Nicolas Breakspear who became the only English Pope as Adrian IV.

As its wealth and influence grew Merton by 1242 held over 200 estates in 16 counties and had daughter houses in Canterbury, Holyrood, Plympton and Taunton. By the time of its dissolution in 1538 it was the second richest Augustinian Priory in England, surpassed only by Cirencester. It is sad to note that, when the priory was "taken over", Henry VIII immediately ransacked it for stone for his Nonsuch Palace nearby at Cheam (3050 cartloads were removed within four months of the dissolution of the Priory).[10] The Palace obliterated Cuddington church - Walter's first benefice. To-day the foundations of Merton

Priory "one of the most powerful and illustrious priories in the history of the Catholic Church in England"[11] lie under the Sainsbury's Savacentre and a newly built link road.

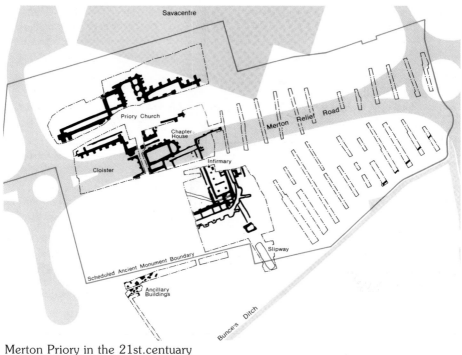

Merton Priory in the 21st.centuary

Oxford - The Emerging University [12]

At the opening of thirteenth century the University was at a critical, even precarious, stage of development. The first serious Town and Gown disturbance occurred in 1208 when a student killed a townswoman, possibly by mistake when practising archery. The townsmen attacked the students and hanged two of them who had no connection with the death. The students and masters fled the town, scattering to Reading, Cambridge, Stamford and Paris. A full settlement of the troubles took place only in 1214 when the excommunication imposed by the Papacy following the King's refusal to accept Stephen Langton as Archbishop was finally lifted. The settlement (brokered by the Papal Legate) established a Chancellor of the University under the jurisdiction of the Bishop of Lincoln and tackled what had been one of the running sores between Town and Gown - the provision of lodgings for students on terms fair to both.This was not the only cause of friction between Town and Gown. It looks as though little has changed over the years. Apart from problems over student lodgings, animosity resulted from rowdiness, drinking, wenching and privilege, the last-named being based in those days on the special position of "clerks" (who were not subject to the common law), and more recently on wealth, class, ostentatious dress and behaviour &c. It is thought that the violent reaction of the Town in the 1208 disturbance was in part due to nationalist feeling against the Papacy over the Archbishop issue.

These causes of friction have always existed. In the previous twelfth century the University had struggled into existence on an unregulated free enterprise basis. While there were famous schools in other centres e.g. Exeter, Northampton and Lincoln, Oxford is said to have been the natural site for the first English University, partly from its excellent communications in the middle of the Kingdom, and partly because of its key political position, with a royal palace (Beaumont Palace) and hunting lodge (Woodstock), and frequent state activities. In England, as in Europe, professors (as we would now call them) moved from place to place, setting themselves up to teach their special subjects and students, often in their early teens, came to sit at their feet. By 1150 a number of teachers were established in Oxford. Further momentum was provided by a major repatriation, on royal instructions, of English professors and students from Paris in 1167.

Some of the students at Oxford paid for themselves (the well-to-do maintaining their own establishment, like the Bek brothers in Halegod's House bought by Walter in 1267 for Merton College), others were financed by rich patrons, both individuals and institutions (like Merton Priory), others again lived from hand to mouth. All were young and unprotected and had to cope with surviving away from their homes as well as doing their best to imbibe the instruction on offer.

To meet this situation there came into existence what may be called "academic lodging houses" where the "landlord" might or might not also be a teaching academic. The students lodged and ate there and went out to seek instruction and amusement. The houses were originally organised on a free enterprise basis, but some measure of regulation came in following the Town & Gown settlement in 1214, and there was a major initiative undertaken in 1229 by Henry III who instructed the sheriffs of Oxford and Cambridge to collaborate with the bishop, the university Chancellor and the municipal authorities to regulate rents of lodgings and impose a measure of discipline. By then the position had been exacerbated by the arrival of many students dispersed from Paris in 1229. The academic lodging houses became known as halls. One only survives to-day, St.Edmund Hall (now converted into a college), the others having either disappeared or been absorbed over the next seven centuries by the "colleges" which started to be established in the second half of the 13th.century.

The precarious state of the emerging University was underpinned by the arrival in Oxford in the early thirteenth century of the friars, who combined charitable work with academic teaching, with great success. The Dominicans arrived in 1221 and were followed by the Franciscans, the Carmelites and later by the Augustinians. The example and success of the friars galvanised the University and inspired others to provide financial assistance for young men attending the University or (as in Walter's case) to design and establish purpose-built institutions for promoting higher education - the Colleges. Bishop Hobhouse in 1859 took the view that Walter's purpose was to "secure for his own order in the Church, for the secular priesthood, the academical benefits which the religious orders were so largely enjoying".[13]

Mauger's Hall

The hall where, according to tradition, Walter lodged in Oxford was Mauger Hall, situated on the East side of the Cornmarket, a few yards North of Carfax. A few details of its history may cast some light on the tradition that Walter did spend some time at Oxford University.[14]

The Hall - probably more correctly Mauger's Hall - stood on the site which subsequently became known as the Cross Inn and more recently the Golden Cross. The site on which the Hall subsequently stood was divided into three: the southern part had a frontage of some 31 feet to the Cornmarket, the middle part about 15 feet. In around 1182 both these parts were owned by one Waleron or Waleran of Cricklade. In about 1189 Waleran gifted the southern part to Osney Abbey and the middle part to Merton Priory. The next development was in about 1193. Osney Abbey built a house on the southern part and granted it to Mauger, who was a vintner, at 4 shillings per annum. The Abbey retained the shops which were on the ground floor fronting the Cornmarket. In the same year Merton Priory granted the middle part for ever to Mauger at an annual rent of 40 shillings.[15]

On this combined plot Mauger established his Hall and also - a few years later, around 1200 - an inn. In 1362 the Hall was acquired by one Gingiver and it was known for a time as Gingiver's Hall. The whole property was eventually acquired by New College, with Merton Priory relinquishing its perpetual rent and interest for £ 20 in around 1531. The buildings now on the Golden Cross site (used mainly as a restaurant and luxury shops) are more recent, the north range being of the fifteenth century and the south range of the second half of the seventeenth century. It is now convenient to marshal the evidence supporting Walter's

The Golden Cross, site of Mauger's Hall

attendance as a student at Oxford. First, a letter survives written by Adam de Marisco (Marsh) to Brother Adam Bechesoveres stating that Walter is making application to the Bishop of Lincoln (Robert Grosseteste) for sub-deacon's orders and commending him as "honorabilis vir"- a worthy man. The letter was addressed to Bechesoveres because he was close to Grosseteste, probably a member of his household. The date of the letter is unknown but Grosseteste was Bishop of Lincoln 1235-1253 and had earlier been one of the first Chancellors of Oxford. Marsh and Grosseteste were both outstanding Oxford scholars. It seems likely that Marsh got to know Walter when he was a student at Oxford and it is possible that he was one of Marsh's pupils.[16]

Quite apart from its evidence in support of an Oxford University connection, this letter unmistakably marks Walter, a clerk of humble origins at Merton Priory in his thirties, as a rising man. Why else should three leading scholars and churchmen take an interest in his application to be ordained as a sub-deacon?

Perhaps more telling on the Oxford issue is the fact that Walter was applying to the Bishop of Lincoln - in whose diocese Oxford lay in those days: in the absence of any Oxford connection it would have been more natural for Walter to apply to the Bishop of Winchester whose diocese covered both Basingstoke in Hampshire and Merton in Surrey.

The fact that Merton College did, eventually, come to be in Oxford may also be cited in support. It is true that the College was originally established at Malden in Surrey, and in the 1262 abortive documentation for the College neither Oxford nor any other university is specifically mentioned. We do not know why - perhaps the unsettled state of the Kingdom - and it has been speculated that Walter, a few years later, was still "hedging his bets" by acquiring some land in

Cambridge: but the fact remains that, in due course, Oxford was the location which Walter picked.

We have already mentioned John of Basing (or Basingstoke), the Greek scholar who had studied at Oxford and was a friend of Grosseteste. Since his family must have been known to Walter's (they may have been related) this may have provided a further impetus towards Oxford.

The close connection between Walter and Osney Abbey (just outside Oxford to the west, near the railway station) has been cited to support Walter's attendance as a student, with the suggestion that he may have lodged there. The evidence for this connection is (1) the close interest taken by the Osney Abbey Chronicler, Thomas Wykes, in Walter's career - his appointment as Bishop of Rochester, the detailed account of his death, and the flowery and enthusiastic obituary verses (printed in Appendix II) (2) the provisions in Walter's will (3) the assistance given by the Abbey to the endowment of Merton College (see chapter 8)

It could be argued that this evidence is equally consistent with a connection with the Abbey established only later in Walter's life. He was frequently in Oxford, attending the Court as a King's Clerk and as Chancellor, and in connection with the establishment of Merton College, and very likely stayed at the Abbey. We have already noted that Mauger's Hall was linked both with Osney Abbey and Merton Priory, so it is perhaps reasonable to conclude that Walter's connection with Osney did originate during his time as a student and continued throughout his life.

Finally, the details, summarised above, of the history of Mauger's Hall do establish a strong connection between Merton Priory and the Hall: if, as we have assumed, Merton Priory decided to send a young protégé to study in Oxford, their tenant Mauger would be the obvious guardian-cum-landlord to take him in.

Merton Priory
The Professional Clerk
(c.1220 - c.1238)

W have assumed that Walter had finished his school, university and legal education by about 1220-25 when he was 20-25 years old. We have also assumed that his professional education/apprenticeship as a "clerk" at Merton Priory took over at that point - part learning and part doing - though it is possible that this had started earlier during breaks from studies in Oxford and/or London. (There were, of course, no formal university terms and vacations in those days, though there may have been a "long vacation" at harvest-time). We speculated, above, as to what skills were being learned, based on the activities which Walter was found to be engaged in later. There is no real modern description of the responsibilities of this kind of "clerk" but the descriptions "Town Clerk" and "Clerk of Works" - still in use to-day - give some flavour of the duties of a senior clerk - a combination of land agent, legal adviser (or "house counsel") and chief operating officer.

It is interesting to note that Henry III paid his first visit to Merton Priory in 1217 when (aged 10) he attended a Peace Conference with the Dauphin of France at nearby Kingston, and accommodation was provided at the Priory. If Walter (then aged around 17) was back at Merton Priory on that occasion it is likely that he had his first meeting with his Royal patron.

Walter first comes to light as a recognised clerk in a series of deeds in the 1225-30 period[1], to which he was one of the witnesses under the description "Walter, the clerk of Basingstoke". In other documents, some into the 1230s, Walter is found as a party, instead of just a witness (for example he acted as attorney to the Prior of Merton, Henry de Basinges), and the description varies slightly e.g. "Walter of Basingstoke", "Walter of Basing, clerk", "Walter the clerk"

overleaf; Mid Surrey

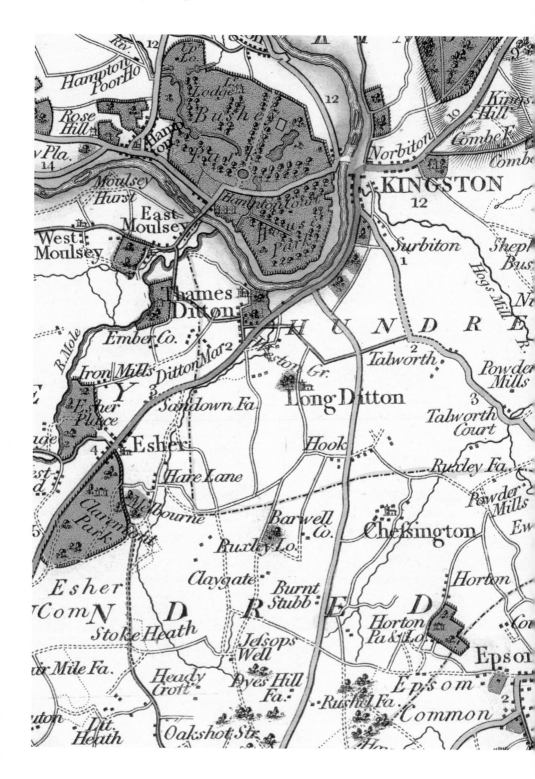

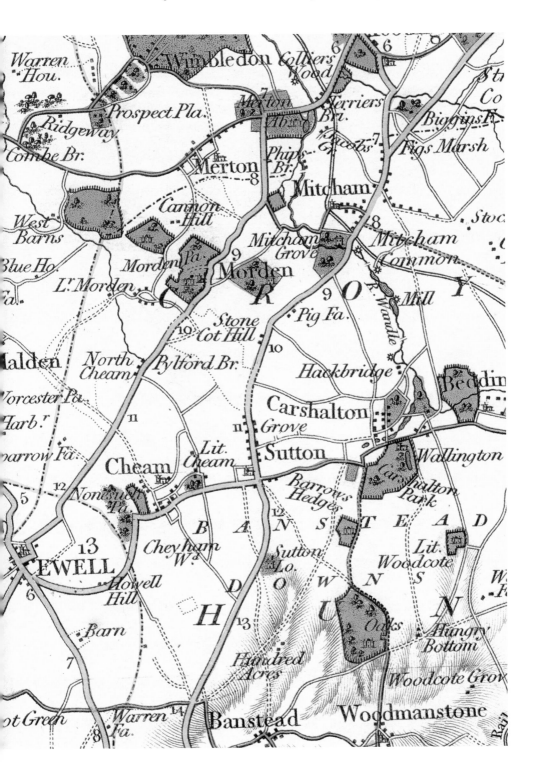

Although our only evidence comes from a small number of formal documents spread over several years Walter must have become very busy on the Priory's behalf. He must also have become very useful since the Prior appointed him to the living of Cuddington in around 1233, his first preferment, when he was about 33 years old. Cuddington is a village one mile north east of Ewell in Surrey: the church was demolished as part of the construction of Henry VIII's Nonsuch Palace at the end of the 1530s, although its foundations, with alterations in the mid thirteenth century i.e. during Walter's time as incumbent, have been traced under the later building.[2]

King Henry paid further visits to Merton Priory in 1230, 1233, 1236 and 1237 and it seems very likely that Walter had some contact, if not with the King himself, with his entourage on one or more of these occasions. It is possible, too, that Walter (as a member of a prominent local family) made a point of being back in Basingstoke on the occasions of the King's visits there in 1226 and 1230.

At some time between 1235 and 1238 Walter was recruited to the Royal service under Chancellor Nevill. The dating of this career change is based on circumstantial evidence summarised below. However, before turning to this new development we can look at Walter's development of his private property portfolio.

The Foundation of Walter's Fortune

In the 1230-40 period Walter found time for his own and his family's affairs. Apart from taking over, subject to his father's life interest, the Fitzace land which came from his mother's family, Walter acquired at least seven properties in and around Basingstoke.[3] These included three parcels in the Rughemede meadow (adjoining the West or Salisbury Field outside the town); property which abutted on the family home, probably including a house for himself; half a yardland i.e.about 15 acres, which came with an easement permitting the erection of stalls in the market; a messuage under the Bell Tower ("clocherium"); and a virgate of land (around 30 acres) in Eastrop (then just outside Basingstoke on the east side, now absorbed into the town) and the Basingstoke open fields. The first witness to this last transaction was the Chancellor Ralph Neville, so Walter would have dealt with him.

Where did Walter get the cash for these transactions? There could have been little surplus income from the family Fitzace estate after providing for his parents until their deaths and before he made over the estate to the Basingstoke Hospital around the end of the decade. Nor is it likely that he received any stipend from Merton Priory. The sources were probably (a) his income from Cuddington from

1233 (b) the fees earned when he joined the Royal Chancery around the 1235-7 period (further discussed below).[4]

In addition to these purchases, in 1240 the King granted the manor of Basingstoke to Walter for five years. Previously, the men of Basingstoke themselves, under a special arrangement with the King, had held the manor, but kept getting into arrears with their rent. It looks as though - as with other property transactions - Walter volunteered (or perhaps the King or his officials asked him) to sort out the mess and, at the same time, by his superior management gain some advantage for himself. In any event the grant of the manor of Basingstoke was an obvious mark of Royal favour for the newly recruited public servant. Further afield, in 1240 Walter began his acquisition of the manors of Malden with Chessington and Farleigh in Surrey, although the title was not finally perfected until 1257. These estates became the original endowment of Merton College in the 1260s. The transaction is described in more detail below (see chapter 5).

Malden Manor House to-day, on the site of Walter's building

The Seven Sisters - and their families

From the mid-1230s Walter arranged property settlements for some of his sisters as they married.[5] Some transactions were direct transfers by Walter: in other cases a third party transfers the property but Walter can be seen to be involved e.g. as a witness, so that his financial backing can be assumed; in other cases again Walter does not appear to participate but one of his brothers-in-law acts as a witness and, again, we venture to assume that Walter was involved.[6]

While describing the marriage settlements for Walter's sisters it will be convenient also to refer to other benefits which Walter arranged for these seven families (even though this will involve projecting forward into the future). We do not know the exact order in which the sisters were married.[7]

Christina

She was probably Walter's oldest sister and she married Thomas de Worting (Worting is a village some 2 miles to the west of Basingstoke) at some time in the late 1230s. There is no record of any property settled on her marriage, perhaps because Thomas was already a landowner.

Their son Thomas junior succeeded to Walter's Manor of Basingstoke Merton (see chapter 7 below) in the early 14th.century when his cousin Walter Oliver died without issue. Thomas junior was also one of the first eight scholars at Merton College, founded by his uncle Walter in the 1260s.

Their daughter Alice married Nicholas Thedden (probably from Thedden Grange near Alton 11 miles south east of Basingstoke) and Walter employed him in his household.

Walter left legacies in his will to his sister Cristina, to Alice, Nicholas and their sons and to Cristina junior, the unmarried daughter.

Alice

She married c.1235 Peter de la Clythe (or de la Clyde). He was probably from Cliddesden, 2 miles south of Basingstoke (spelled Clydesden in the 13th.century)[8]. It appears that Walter settled on them the half a yardland (around 15 acres), which included an easement permitting the erection of stalls in the Basingstoke Market, referred to above.[9].

Their eldest son Peter de la Clythe II was one of Walter's six co-heirs (and thus succeeded to a share of his real property on his death). Three other sons, John, William and Roger were among the eight original scholars at Merton College.

Walter presented John to the living of Sutton in the diocese of Bath and Wells in 1266 and left him by his will £ 150 (some £ 150,000 in 2000 money), four silver salvers and a silver footless cup.

Perhaps harking back to the property settled on Alice's marriage, the 1274 Inquisition of Edward I (into Royal interests in Basingstoke) includes a complaint that Peter de la Clythe (probably Walter's brother-in-law) had built a house encroaching on the market- place "where the fish carts are wont to stand".[10]

Castania

She married c.1236 Richard Oliver or Elvet (perhaps from Elvetham 9 miles east north east from Basingstoke). There were three property transactions about this time in Richard's favour (one jointly with his brother), involving 20 acres spread around the Basingstoke fields, two messuages in Basingstoke and a meadow in

Fridmede (north of the town), in which Walter's involvement can be assumed. In addition some years later, in the 1260s, Walter settled his manor of Basingstoke Merton on Walter Oliver, the younger son of Castania and Richard, but he appears to have died without issue, and the estate passed to his first cousin Thomas de Worting junior.

Their elder son Richard Oliver was one of Walter's six co-heirs. He became rector of Hunington (Hannington near Kingsclere, 7 miles north west of Basingstoke), no doubt with help from Walter.

The younger son, Walter, was one of the first eight scholars of Merton College.

Edith
She was married twice, first c.1237-8 to Robert Eddrad, and, secondly, around 1255, to Thomas Tayllard. In the early 1240s, when Walter held the manor of Basingstoke, he was able to transfer to Edith and Robert some land in Basingstoke. Two other transactions occurred at around the same time (in which Walter's hand can be assumed), involving the transfer to Robert of 1 1/2 acres near the road to Cliddesden (south east of the town) and land in Basingstoke with a capital messuage and meadow. Later, at an unknown date, there is a transfer (in which Walter's involvement can again be assumed) of land in Basingstoke to Edith, by then the wife of Thomas Tayllard.

Walter left legacies to Edith, to her eldest son (Robert Eddrad II), to her unmarried daughter to establish her in the nunnery at Wilton, and to her son by Thomas Tayllard (Roger).

Thomas Tayllard served in Walter's household, as did his brother (also named Roger).

Agnes
In 1239 she married Gilbert Ewell (Fitz Osbert), a "thriving yeoman" from Walter's new parish of Cuddington in Surrey.[11] Walter bought two Surrey estates in Cuddington and Ewell (from John Blanch and William Ballard) and settled them on the couple.[12] One of these transactions involved Walter treating with Richard Neville, the Chancellor since 1226, since he held the fee of the Ewell estate which had escheated to the Crown.

Of their three sons, the eldest, William, became a canon of St. Pauls and Sarum (no doubt with help from Walter): he was the chief executor of Walter's will and the main family legatee.

The other two sons, Robert and Philip, were among the original eight scholars of Merton College.

Their daughter, Agnes junior, married Robert FitzNigell junior, son of a "Montfortian" (of the same name) who was compelled to transfer lands to Walter for the endowment of Merton College in 1265 by way of compensation for damage done to Walter's property during the baronial troubles.

Walter left legacies to his sister Agnes and to her son Philip. To the eldest son, William, Walter left his bible and a mazer cup, and a legacy of £ 300 (some £ 300,000 in 2000 money).

Walter also left to Robert FitzNigell junior all his interest in his father's lands plus a legacy to assist in restoring them; together with other legacies to relations of Robert.

Matilda I
She married John Wyly (probably from the Wiltshire village of that name, 10 miles north west of Salisbury). They had a daughter, Clara, and three sons, John, Hugo and William who were employed by Walter in his household. There is no record of any property transaction involving Walter.

Matilda II
We have no indication as to why two daughters were both named Matilda. Matilda II married one Stak' or Stake atte Wich', who probably came from Farlington in the hinterland behind Portsmouth, since a family of that name held the manor of Stake in the mid-13th. Century[13]: Wich' was probably Wickham, spelled Wicham in mediaeval times, a town about 7 miles north west of Farlington[14], and in 1324 the birth place of William of Wykeham, founder of Winchester College and New College, Oxford.

Here, too, there is no record of any property transaction involving Walter, but Matilda's son Alan Stak (or Portsmue, the mediaeval spelling for Portsmouth) was one of Walter's six co-heirs and thus received an interest in his real property on his death.

Matilda II's younger son, Walter Portsmue, followed his uncle as parson of Cuddington.

We can now pick up on Walter's recruitment to the Royal service.

Royal Service -
The First Phase (c. 1235 - c. 1242)

IN A DOCUMENT dated to 1237/38 Walter was described as "Walter de Merton". He was also described in this way in the famous letter (already referred to) written by Adam de Marisco (Marsh) to Brother Adam Bechesovers supporting Walter's claims for ordination as a sub-deacon by the Bishop of Lincoln. While no firm date is available for this letter the scholarly view is that it could have been written as early as 1235, the year in which Robert Grosseteste became Bishop of Lincoln. Describing Walter as "de Merton" suggests either that he had left the Priory or that he had taken on other official responsibilities elsewhere, so his transfer to the Royal Service might - on that basis - be assigned to 1235 or shortly thereafter.

In May 1238 the Close Rolls record an inquisition, subsequently confirmed by a Royal charter, into Walter's property at Basingstoke, for the purpose of establishing the correct rent (payable to the Crown) for these holdings. It also, incidentally, is an important source of information as to the family and its property. (As a result of the inquisition the rent was reduced)

In August 1238 Walter acquired from Henry de Brayboeuf (a Hampshire knight, the Lord of Eastrop Manor) a virgate of land with appurtenances in Eastrop and the fields of Basingstoke. The first witness was "Ralph (Neville), Bishop of Chichester, the King's Chancellor".

As already noted, in 1239 Walter was involved in negotiations with Ralph Neville, the Chancellor, over the purchase of an estate in Ewell.

Scholarly analysis of these transactions - particularly the Ewell estate deeds and the Basingstoke inquisition (and its confirmation by Royal charter) - strongly suggest that Walter was by then working in the Royal Chancery and was thus both familiar with the special documentation involved and able to call on procedures available under Royal authority to consolidate his personal and family possessions.[1] The circumstantial evidence provided by these property transactions would place Walter's recruitment a year or two later, around 1236-7.

However, the first positive record of Walter's activities in the Royal service (apart from these private transactions) is not until 1240 when, with a Peter Tany, he was charged with reviewing the Royal demesnes i.e. the estates held directly by the Crown, in Kent, Essex, Hertfordshire and Middlesex. The territory to be covered was large, and the instructions were drawn in great detail, so it must have been a major undertaking.[2] Notwithstanding, in the same year, 1240, Walter found time to embark on one of his major acquisitions, purchasing estates owned by a new colleague who was involved in the review of the Royal demesne, William Watevill.[3] This appears to be a typical example of Walter's entrepreneurial flair - spotting that a new colleague has financial problems, helping him by sorting them out and at the same time acquiring valuable property on terms advantageous to himself.

Watevill's estates were the manors of Malden, with Chessington, and Farleigh, all in Surrey, quite close to each other and about 12 miles south west of Westminster. There were many limited interests in the properties and also a charge in favour of a Jewish moneylender.

Vacating these interests required much skilful negotiation, conveyancing and litigation, plus considerable perseverance - displaying Walter's talents to the full. The title was not finally perfected until around 1257 - some 17 years later. In 1264 Walter acquired the advowson of Malden church from Merton Priory and transferred it to Merton College.

Malden Church, the oldest part in the left foreground

As we will see Malden became Walter's "base" and the administrative HQ of Merton College in its initial phase. The manor house at Malden (on the same site as its predecessor in Walter's day) is conveniently about 3 miles from Chessington and about 4 miles from Merton Priory. The manors of Malden with Chessington and Farleigh formed the original endowment of Merton College.

Returning to 1240, we have no other indication of Walter's activities in the Royal Chancery around that date, and indeed within one or two years he transferred his skills (temporarily as it turned out) to the Bishop of Durham, Nicholas Farnham. However, before describing this development we must take note of Walter's first major charitable endowment - for the Hospital of St.John the Baptist at Basingstoke.

The Basingstoke Hospital

It has been suggested that the Hospital was already in existence (apparently on the basis that most towns had one)[4] but this suggestion appears to be rejected, effectively by Walter himself. In a grant of land to the "house of St.John the Baptist at Basingstoke", dated to around 1240, the parties declared "Not only are the seals of the aforesaid parties alternately placed to this chirograph, but for the security of it they have procured the placing upon it of the seal of Sir Walter de Merton, the first founder of the said house". The grantor was Thomas le Forester, an associate of Walter's (and a beneficiary under his will by a legacy of 50 shillings), so the statement as to "first founder" is very specific.[5]

If Walter was indeed re-endowing an existing Hospital we do not know where it was situated before Walter's involvement.

Walter's endowment (or foundation) took place around 1240. Most accounts assign it to the period 1240-1250 but it seems to have occurred soon after the death of his father (his mother had died earlier), and the 1238 Inquisition into Walter's property in Basingstoke assumes that both his parents are dead. In the charter to the Hospital he stated that he was acting "in memory of the laudable life of Lady Christina my mother" and he laid upon the brethren of the Hospital the obligation to maintain in the parish church of St.Michael the two wax candles which his mother and father had ordained should be lit there in perpetuity for the celebration of divine service.

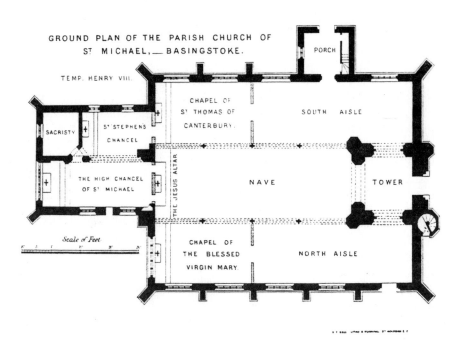

GROUND PLAN OF THE PARISH CHURCH OF
St MICHAEL, — BASINGSTOKE.

St.Michael's, Basingstoke: St.Stephen's Chapel in the south east corner

There is a tradition that the Merton chantry was in St.Stephen's chapel in the parish church, sited in what is now the South Chancel Aisle.[6] It is possible that it was in this chapel - the oldest part of St.Michael's Church - that Walter's parents were buried. In 1494-5 one Edward Cooke directed that he should be buried in this chapel and in 1517 one John Cooke left the same directions.[7] Were they perhaps related to Walter's father ?

The foundation of the Hospital was effected by two (undated) deeds executed, it appears, with only a short interval between, and with few differences in the text, mainly in the definition of the beneficiaries and the extent of the property transferred to the Hospital. This is plausibly explained by Walter's father dying after the first deed (his mother had died some time before), so that "vacant possession" of the family home became available.[8]

The beneficiaries were originally to be poor and sick travellers, but to them were added (by the second deed) ailing priests, and later - when the Hospital was brought under the umbrella of Merton College - aged and infirm fellows of the College as well.

The charter transfers "the entire property which the late William le Cok held of my ancestors in Basingstoke and also the entire house which belonged to the aforesaid William and the house called St.John's in the same town ...to found in the same a hospital".

The site of the Hospital is known - it was not demolished until the late 18th.century - but it is not wholly clear what land and buildings were transferred by Walter. The description in the charter appears to indicate (a) a house with land i.e. the Fitzace inheritance in which Walter's father had a life interest, and (b) another house i.e.the one called St.John's, which is thought to refer to the house transferred by the first deed. Were they all in one block? We know from other sources, discussed above, about the Fitzace inheritance, and that Walter acquired other property in and around Basingstoke in the 1230-40 period. One particular acquisition suggests that Walter had a property abutting on the family home, probably with a house of his own. There are further uncertainties. The charter suggests that the transfer is of a site to be used for the Hospital, not an endowment to generate income to support it. However, the Fitzace inheritance included agricultural land in "the fields": was this intended to be included? If so - which seems likely ("the entire property ....of my ancestors in Basingstoke") - there was also an element of endowment. Was "the house called St John's" one of the properties acquired by Walter, independently of the Fitzace inheritance?

While these details are not altogether clear, the tradition is that Walter established the Hospital in the family mansion in Basingstoke, and we have no reason to challenge this.

It is evident that by the time of his endowment Walter had achieved, both locally and further afield in England, sufficient standing to generate other donations to the Hospital, certainly of land and no doubt of money and personal property as well. It is intriguing to note that a number of these land transfers were to the sisters as well as the brethren of the Hospital, although there is no reference to them in the charter itself.[9]

The Hospital also attracted Royal support. In 1251-2 Henry III granted letters of protection to the Hospital. In 1253 the King granted a right of a perpetual chantry in the chapel of the Hospital, and in 1262 he formally took the Hospital founded by "our beloved clerk and friend Walter de Merton, Canon of Wells" under royal protection. The royal re-foundation was in turn approved by the Papal Legate Cardinal Ottobon in 1268: he granted it freedom from episcopal control provided that the chapel was not prejudicial to the mother church. Henry III also granted the Hospital perpetual freedom from taxation and payment of subsidies. Royal support was continued by Edward I and subsequent monarchs.

The first warden of the Hospital was Henry Cardyff, the parson of Eastrop, a village just outside Basingstoke to the north east, and the second was Peter de Abingdon, a lifelong friend and colleague of Walter's, who subsequently became the first warden of Merton College.

It has been suggested that the transfer to Royal patronage in 1262 was engineered by Walter to offset problems in its management - which the wording hints at ("with a pious desire that an authoritative act of our Royal bounty should supply what could not, in this respect, be fulfilled by himself") - or alternatively to protect the endowment from Walter's political enemies in the baronial party.

The Statutes governing Merton College of 1264, 1270 and 1274 link the Hospital closely to the College and make the College responsible for its support.

By his will Walter left 450 marks for the purchase of more land and a further 100 marks for the employment of a chaplain. These legacies were duly paid after his death in 1277, and 176 acres were purchased in Basingstoke and Iwood (north east of Basingstoke, between the town and Basing) in 1283-4. It is interesting to note from this transaction an average price per acre of £1 14s.

There are records of several infirm fellows of Merton College retiring to the Hospital in the fourteenth and fifteenth centuries.[10]

Despite the promising beginning, the widespread support, its re-launch as a Royal foundation and the link with Merton College, the Hospital faded after its first centenary. It was failing by the sixteenth century, became derelict and was replaced by Merton Farmhouse in the eighteenth century. Its endowments appear to have been merged into the College's after the Dissolution, when the Hospital was taken over by the Court of Augmentations but was then returned to the College by Edward VI.

Why did the Hospital not prosper? On the face of it because the College neglected it. First, "Very soon after its foundation the college threw the maintenance of the chapel services on the lessee of the hospital estate"[11]; and, secondly, there does not seem to have been too much supervision of the lessees to see whether they were carrying out their obligations. In 1401 Henry IV ordered an inquisition as to the state of the Hospital. It was found that, while the warden of the hospital was bound to find and maintain a chaplain, a clerk and two poor people, in fact in the last six years, there had been no clerk and no poor inmates. The Warden of Merton, as ex officio warden of the Hospital, was found to have been in default and the revenues were seized by the Crown and not released until 1405.[12]   The practice of "contracting out" the duties to lessees, however, continued until around 1700.

It is perhaps surprising to find that the Hospital was only intended to accommodate two poor persons plus the very occasional incapacitated fellow of the College, and that its chapel measured internally only 12 feet x 5 feet. [13] Walter's legacy of 100 marks was to provide in perpetuity for the chaplain, while his larger legacy of 450 marks, his original gift of the family estate and the gifts from others, must have given the Hospital at least 250 acres of agricultural land, plus two houses with gardens, orchards &c.[14] This endowment plus the ministrations of a warden, a chaplain and a clerk (and no doubt some servants) would seem to be more than adequate for looking after two poor people and funding the annual visits of the Warden or a Fellow of Merton, as provided for in the leases.

However, without a knowledge of fluctuations in costs and agricultural yields (and the demand for accommodation for the travelling poor, sick persons &c.) it is not possible to understand the full position. Clearly, after the departure of Walter and Peter de Abingdon there would not have been the same emotional attachment to Basingstoke and the Fitzace family home. It looks as though, from a College viewpoint, the Hospital was something of a distraction, so that it made sense to "contract out" the duties against some diminution in rent. In removing the charitable object, the Dissolution eliminated this side-show and the Basingstoke estate became a conventional agricultural holding of the College.

Serving the Prince Bishop
(c.1241/2 - c.1247) [1]

We do not know how Walter moved to Nicholas Farnham's service at Durham. Walter may have met Nicholas in the Royal household (where he served as the Royal physician) or the link may have been Merton Priory, since Nicholas held the Priory living of Long Ditton (some 6 miles south west of Merton)[2].

There must have been some understanding between the Royal advisers and the Bishop as to the transfer - perhaps it was felt important to provide Nicholas, who was something of an academic, with a strong "supporting team". (There is an echo of some such arrangement in a letter from Henry III to the Bishop - date unknown - in which he referred to Walter as "our and your beloved clerk")

Nicholas was an outstanding scholar who had studied originally at Oxford, became professor of medicine at Paris (and also taught dialectics, physics and theology), and then became professor of medicine at Bologna. Returning to England in 1229 he taught logic and natural philosophy at Oxford and became physician to Henry III. He was appointed to Durham in 1241 and retired in 1248, surviving a further 9 years thereafter. His main achievements as Bishop appear to have been pushing on with the building of the cathedral and the reconstruction of Finchale Priory (3 1/2 miles north east of Durham).

Nicholas Farnham did indeed have about him in Durham a strong team, including a large contingent of Surrey and Hampshire men. There were (in addition to Walter) some outstanding individuals like William Kilkenny, later Bishop of Ely and Chancellor. Walter is recorded as acting as a judge in the Palatinate Court in 1242, and by the end of that year he was acting as the Bishop's Chancellor, effectively his chief executive. In 1246 Walter, with other of the Bishop's staff, came south to Sussex to complete a transaction on behalf of Hexham Abbey.

Durham Cathedral

In the same year, 1246, the Pope (Innocent IV) granted Walter "Chancellor of the Bishop of Durham" permission to hold an additional benefice provided that he relinquished another which he held. This is the first Papal notice taken of Walter and marks him as "a rising man". It is not clear to which livings the Papal authority refers: Walter had acquired Cuddington around 1233, and no other benefice is known at that time - his next appointment was in the following year

The Durham Skyline - Cathedral and Castle

1247, to Sedgefield (see below). The general rule was that no one might hold more than one "cure of souls" without Church authority, but this did not apply to sinecures like cathedral appointments. It appears that the rule was not rigidly enforced in England until Archbishop Peckham's appointment in 1279.[3]

Walter's work for Bishop Farnham must have been very satisfactory since substantial, additional patronage within the Durham diocese came his way about this time. First was the church of Sedgefield, some 8 miles north west of Stockton Co. Durham, which Walter acquired some time after 1247. Since the rector was also the Lord of the Manor this was a very rich living. The oldest part of the church now standing - the nave - dates from Walter's time, around 1245; and most of the remainder (except the tower) was built by 1300.

Second was Staindrop, 8 miles south west of Bishop's Auckland in the same county, which Walter obtained by 1253. This is an outstanding church, sometimes to-day described as "the Cathedral of the Dales" with pre-conquest features, a 12th. Century nucleus in the nave and much of the remainder built in the first half of the 13th. Century.

St.Edmund's, Sedgefield

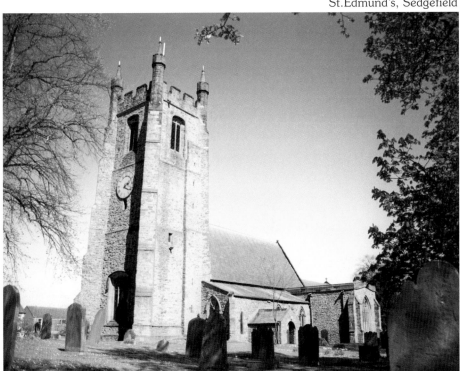

Third was Haltwhistle (in mediaeval times Hautwisel - the meeting of the streams by the hill), 16 miles west of Hexham, to which Walter was appointed by 1253. This too is a fine Early English parish church largely completed by 1250,

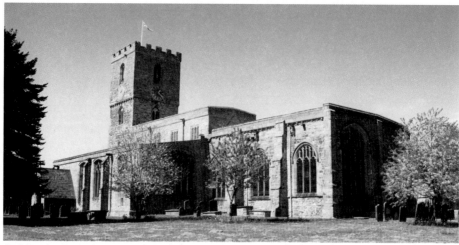

St.Mary's, Staindrop

Holy Cross, Haltwhistle

though Walter must have been carrying out improvements or repairs some 10 years later - since in 1262 the King gave Walter two oak trees "for his church at Hautwisel".

While the records are not completely clear it appears that, at Sedgefield and Staindrop, Walter arranged for his Ewell, Elvet/Oliver and de la Clythe kinsmen to succeed him.

Walter did not obtain authority for these additional holdings.

Walter was also active on his own behalf. In 1247/8 he purchased the manor of Stillington, 5 miles south of Sedgefield from the Amundeville family, the price including discharge of debts to a Jewish moneylender from York.[2] (This was one of a number of similar transactions which Walter undertook: he was an expert in the special, detailed jurisdiction governing Jewish moneylending and property holding)

During his time in Durham Walter must have established good relations with the Dominican friaries at Newcastle and Hartlepool since he remembered both of them in his will

In about 1247-8 Walter returned to the royal service, based in London, but following the Court around the country. Like his earlier move to the north this transfer must also have been "arranged". Bishop Farnham resigned in 1249.

Before leaving Durham we must note the suggestion [5] that Walter gained the inspiration for founding a college of higher education for the secular clergy during his time serving Bishop Farnham.

Mr. Alexander Murray argues that not only Merton College but also University and Balliol Colleges can trace their roots to Durham.[6] This theory is ingeniously constructed around the person of William of Durham (sometimes Sedgefield). There are three stages.

(1) William, an Englishman, was born in 1188, probably at Sedgefield (to which we have seen that Walter was appointed c.1247). He may have attended Oxford University but by around 1220 he was a Professor of Theology in Paris. In 1229 he left Paris with other English masters and students and appeared in 1235 as an archdeacon in or near Caen. Shortly afterwards he was elected Archbishop of Rouen but declined the post in view of opposition and in 1238 returned to England to become rector of Bishop's Wearmouth, now part of Sunderland. In the last year of his life (1248-9) he took a case to the Curia at Lyons and on his way back re-visited Rouen where he died. He left money to

the University of Oxford which was the original endowment of University College.

(2) During William's time in France (c.1220 - c.1240) there was a quickening interest in establishing colleges of higher education, particularly directed to training the clergy. The College des Bons-Enfants was founded in 1209, the College of St. Thomas in 1219, the College des Dix-huit in 1231 and the Sorbonne was started around 1254.

(3) William absorbed and promoted this enthusiasm, both during his time at Rouen and on his return to the diocese of Durham. At Rouen he directly or indirectly inspired William of Sanaa, a canon of Rouen from around 1250 (and subsequently elected Archbishop of Rouen but blocked on grounds of pluralism) to found a further theological college in Paris. Back at Wearmouth he was intimate with the Bishop's circle and generated a similar inspiration. (Walter, as we have seen, served there from 1241/2 - 1247). Bishop Farnham resigned in 1249 and was succeeded by Walter Kirkham. Bishop Kirkham was not a university man but nonetheless in 1260 he imposed upon John Balliol the somewhat unusual penance which resulted in the formation of Balliol College, having adopted the educational enthusiasm which had been planted at Durham by William.

Bearing in mind the internationalism of the mediaeval Church (to-day we might speak of its "global vision"), the close relationship between leading churchmen and scholars, and the energy with which they promoted ideas calculated to benefit the Church, Mr. Murray's closely argued case is convincing and there is no reason to doubt that William and those with whom he worked shared and fostered this educational enthusiasm.

So far as Walter is concerned, by the time that he was recruited to Durham (1241/2) he had already built up his manor of Basingstoke Merton, set up settlements for sisters as they married, founded and endowed the Basingstoke Hospital, and initiated the purchase of the Watevill estate, and he went on to acquire the Amundeville estate while serving in Durham. It is reasonable to assume that he had already, in his 40s., decided to apply his accumulating wealth to endow some additional good cause: he had established the Hospital to help the travelling poor and the sick and ailing priests, so, with nephews and cousins appearing in considerable numbers, who could benefit from a good start in life, something educational was on the cards. It could well be that William of Durham inspired him to graft the postgraduate training of priests onto a scheme for general education which was already forming in his mind.

As Mr. Murray points out, finding a common source at Durham for the three premier Oxford colleges side-steps the unedifying competition over which was the first. Without reopening the contest, it is, however, possible to differentiate between the provision of money - in the case of University and Balliol Colleges - and the direct establishment of endowed institutions, with written constitutions, as exemplified by William Sanaa's College in Paris and Walter's Merton College.

Royal Service -
The Second Phase
(c.1247 - 1274)

As we have seen, Walter returned to the Royal service in around 1247-8. In a grant to him of free warren in the demesne lands of Malden by the King in 1249 he is described as clericus noster, "our clerk".[1] We have no details of Walter's employment for the next few years, and it seems probable that he served in the Chancery under William Kilkenny, becoming prothonotarius or senior clerk.[2] In 1255 Henry Wingham was appointed Chancellor and Walter was then definitely recognised as one of the King's Clerks.[3]

Before describing this development, however, we will digress to discuss a major property initiative which has, to date, received little attention.

The Manor of Basingstoke Merton
(Sometimes "Taulkes" or "Watermartens")

The existence of this manor, separate from that of Basingstoke, has been known and because of its name and the fact that it was found in the hands of Thomas de Worting (Walter's nephew, son of his sister Cristina) early in the 14th. Century it could be conjectured that it was another example of Walter's generosity to his sisters' families.[4] Its origin was not, however, established, probably because it was assumed (incorrectly, as now appears) that Walter transferred all, or almost all, his Basingstoke property to the Hospital in around 1240.[5]

Recent research by Mrs Anne Hawker of Basingstoke has uncovered much more, although the exact area and extent of the manorial land have yet to be established.[6] The nucleus of the manor appears to have been the various properties in and around Basingstoke which Walter acquired in the 1230s, which we have already described (less any of that land which Walter transferred to the Hospital, possibly the property and house abutting on the family home).[7] At some stage Walter's landholding was formally recognised as a manor with its own court, distinct from the manor of Basingstoke. Within the town it probably occupied the area north of an east-west line formed by Flaxfield Road, Cross Street and Potters Lane, but excluding St.Michael's Church, the glebe land and the Hospital.

The mansion house was, it appears, the property known as Taukes (the family of Tauke or Tawke succeeded to the manor, as we shall see) and subsequently as Bedford House, which was built by William Russell (Recorder of Basingstoke 1745-61) in the 18th. Century and demolished only in the 1960s to accommodate the new "Town Centre". The site lies to the east of Church Street opposite Church Square, and to-day is under Marks & Spencer's store.

The manor farmhouse, Mrs. Hawker has deduced, was probably the building to-day known as Church Cottage - though only acquired by the Church comparatively recently in the 18th. Century by an exchange - which still stands south west of St. Michael's Church and is used for church and public meetings.

Walter's Manor Farmhouse, now called Church Cottage

It is thought that the additional properties acquired by Walter from the King in 1256 - the meadow of Frithmede (just north of the town by the River Loddon) and the marsh of Iwood (north east of the town) also became part of the manor.[8]

We can speculate that the recognition by King Henry of Basingstoke Merton as a separate manor occurred some time after Walter completed his five year's as grantee of the manor of Basingstoke in 1245 - perhaps to mark his success in putting its affair onto a regular footing. A Royal Charter of 1256, in which the King confirms the grant of the farm of Basingstoke manor to the men of the town for £ 80 p.a.in perpetuity, continues "Reserving to ourselves the farm of the lands of our beloved clerk Walter de Merton which they were formerly wont to render to our Exchequer for his Manor and reserving to the said Walter and his heirs the lands and liberties which he has in the said manor". This seems to indicate that Basingstoke Merton was well established as a separate manor by 1256.[9]

The existence of the separate manor continued to be recognised by the Crown; see a grant in 1319 by Edward II to his brother Edmund, Earl of Kent of "The annual fee farm rent of the manor and town of Basingstoke with the hundred, and the rent of the holding which formerly belonged to Walter de Merton in the same town..."

There are indications in the Basingstoke manorial court, the View of Frankpledge, supporting the concept of the separate jurisdiction of the manorial court of Basingstoke Merton. For example, on 7th. May 1541 three men were accused and fined for carrying ale, loaves and meat "against the assize" out of the jurisdiction and liberty of the manor of Water Martens. Presumably the requirements on price and/or quality were less stringent in the Merton jurisdiction, or perhaps were not being enforced at all.[10]

In the Inquisition of Edward I in 1274 (relating to royal interests in Basingstoke) the jury reported that Walter de Merton had the right to the assize of bread and ale in the town of Basingstoke and that no legal basis for this was known. This may be describing (inaccurately) Walter's authority within his own manor, rather than a right to this assize throughout the whole of the town.

As recently as 1936 Mr. J.R. Ellaway, a well-known local historian, was reported as stating that only 100 years ago "the town was divided into Soke and Upland, all below Flaxfield, Cross Street and Potters Lane was Soke".[11]

The judicial power of the manorial courts - both Basingstoke and Basingstoke Merton - was presumably superseded by the Charter of James I in 1622 which appointed justices to hold a weekly court in the town.

In 1262-3 Walter settled the manor of Basingstoke Merton on Walter Oliver son of Richard Oliver and his heirs and in default of heirs to Thomas de Worting nephew of the said Walter Merton.[12] Walter Oliver is presumably the son of Walter's sister Castania by Richard Elvet, (sometimes Oliver) who would have been between 15 and 30 in 1264: he was one of the first eight scholars at Merton College. He must have died without issue as Basingstoke Merton is found next in Edward II's time (1307-27) in the hands of Thomas de Worting (the younger) the son of Walter's sister Cristina by Thomas de Worting senior. Thomas de Worting junior left a daughter and heiress Maud who married a William Tauke, who thus succeeded to the Manor. In a survey of Basingstoke landholdings (undated but assigned to around 1409) a William Tauke had 297 1/2 acres in and around Basingstoke: most, if not all, came from the de Wortings, and so a substantial proportion from the manor of Basingstoke Merton.[13]

The subsequent descent of the land by inheritance and sale can be traced down to the present.

It is interesting to note that Walter's settlement of Basingstoke Merton did not provide for Richard Oliver junior, Walter Oliver's brother, to succeed on Walter's failure of issue. Richard became Rector of Hannington, no doubt with help from Walter, but only benefited directly from his wealth by being co-heir to Walter in respect of his real estate. Walter obviously considered the de Wortings more deserving.

The death of Walter Oliver without issue (which triggered the remainder to his cousin Thomas de Worting junior) may be echoed by a transaction in around 1280, when his brother Richard Oliver transferred all his land in Basingstoke and Iwode (the marshy pasture north east of the town) in perpetuity to Master Peter de Abingdon (the Warden of the Basingstoke Hospital) "rendering yearly a rose on the feast of St. John the Baptist for all services". At about the same time i.e. 1280, Peter de Abingdon transferred to the Hospital all the land which had been gifted to him by Richard Oliver.[14]

We may now return to Walter's second period of Royal service.

The King's Clerks

The King's Clerks were a corps d'elite among the senior servants and advisers of the King in the reigns of Henry III and Edward I. They came from many different sources and backgrounds (often of comparatively humble origin) but they were recruited and promoted for their abilities, their achievements and their loyalty. Unlike modern, specialised public servants, they were employed at home and abroad on a totally unpredictable variety of tasks. Those who performed well were richly rewarded, with stipends, board and lodging, perquisites, the fees payable by citizens who used the public services which they managed, ecclesiastical and other preferment, and they were permitted, if not encouraged, to amass private wealth while in the Royal service. The most famous of the King's Clerks were Robert Burnell, Chancellor and best-loved servant to Edward I, who acquired 82 manors in 19 counties (and a number of illegitimate children); John

Mansel, Henry III's favourite clerk and "private secretary", who was said to have held over 300 benefices - and Walter himself.

We have already noted that by 1255 Walter was definitely a King's Clerk. He may already have been singled out to represent or act as deputy for the Chancellor. Bishop Hobhouse draws attention to letters written by the Bishops of St. Andrews and Glasgow in 1254-5 in which they describe Walter as "Cancellarius Regis" (the King's Chancellor).[15] It is clear that he was not in fact Chancellor at that time - and the King's grant of the marsh of Ywood in the next year 1256 confirms this, describing Walter simply as "our beloved clerk" - so the Bishops may be describing the de facto position as they saw it from Scotland.

In the same year, 1255, Walter was awarded a complete outfit of clothing - there must have been some uniform style - as a King's Clerk. (He was to be awarded a robe as Chancellor, too, in 1261).[16]

The King also was generous with gifts of game and timber. Walter received gifts of venison in 1255, 1256, 1257, 1258, 1262 (two occasions) and 1272.[17] The minimum gift was two carcases and on one occasion he received six. Timber was given by the King to help with building and repair projects - and must have been very valuable to the recipient. In 1256 Walter received 2 oaks from Woodstock and 7 from Pamber (probably for rebuilding the Basingstoke Hospital); 2 oaks in 1262 from Tadley (suitable for the repair work being carried out at Basingstoke - no doubt on the Hospital) and a further 2 from Pamber; 2 oaks in the same year 1262 from Inglewood (for "his church at Hautwisel"); and in 1268 8 oaks from somewhere near the River Trent for the construction of the scholars' houses and church at Oxford.[18]

In 1257 Walter was appointed to the living of Potton, in Bedfordshire, 11 miles east of Bedford. His appointment to the living of Branston in Lincolnshire, 3 miles south east of Lincoln, probably also took place at about this time.

In 1258 Chancellor Wingham was absent sick on at least two occasions [19] and Walter acted as temporary keeper of the seal and thereafter was Wingham's normal deputy. In the same year the King employed Walter to negotiate with the Papal Legate the terms on which the Pope would grant to Edmund, Earl of Lancaster, the King's son, the Kingdom of Sicily.[20]

In 1259 the King appointed Walter to a vacant prebend in St.Paul's, which carried the right to a house off Paternoster Row close to the Cathedral. It was originally linked to Kentish Town but it was in 1262 exchanged for Holywell/Finsbury, both then villages to the north of London.[21] In the same year Walter was also appointed a canon of Exeter Cathedral and to the living of

Barningham, probably in Suffolk (as he was presented by the Abbey of Bury St. Edmund's - there are several villages of that name). About the same time he was appointed Archdeacon of Bath and subsequently a canon of Wells Cathedral.

Bath Abbey

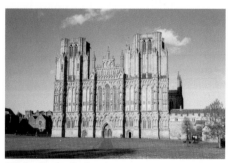

Wells Cathedral

Exeter Cathedral

In 1259 Henry III went to France to seek a general settlement with Louis IX and the great seal went with him while the exchequer seal was left in Walter's care. The King kept in touch with Walter by letter.

The following Spring, in March 1260, the King, alarmed by reports from England, sent secret instructions with the Justiciar, Hugo le Bigod, to England to summon 100 Royal supporters with their knights to London to meet the King in three weeks time.[22] The list is headed by three bishops, two abbots and seven earls ("comites"), and there follow some 90 magnates from all over the country. In 48 hours Walter and his staff had to prepare and seal all the writs requiring attendance on the King and send them in batches to the sheriffs for distribution.

Later in 1260 Nicholas of Ely was appointed Chancellor by the baronial council and Walter disappears from view until the following summer when the King's party regained the upper hand. Nicholas then surrendered the seal to the King who at once handed it to Walter, making him Chancellor.[23] This was on 12th. July 1261. Were it not for the tussle between the King and the Barons Walter might well have achieved this glittering prize some years earlier. Walter's stipend as Chancellor was 400 marks per year, around £ 267 (approximately £ 250,000 in current terms: see the discussion in chapter 11). The King also relieved his "King's Clerk and Chancellor" of all taxes on 50 tuns of wine which Walter imported in that year.[24]

In 1262 the King appointed Walter to the living of Preston-in-Amounderness, in Lancashire.[25] About the same time Walter was also appointed a canon of Salisbury cathedral, with a prebend at Yatesbury, though this was exchanged in the next year for another prebend at Salisbury, that of Bere and Charminster.[26] In the same year, 1262, there is a letter written to Walter by John Mansel, the King's secretary, who

Salisbury Cathedral. It had only been completed in its original form in 1258, about 4 years before Walter's appointment

was travelling with his master in his French dominions.[27] It seeks an update on events in England and illustrates the complete reliance placed by the absent King on his Chancellor.

Again, in 1262, the King found time to relieve Walter of debt of £ 40 which he owed to the Crown.[28] This arose from a transaction in 1260 under which Walter acquired the wardship of the lands and heirs of one William de Meualing against a fine of £ 40. In the course of 1262 Henry III wrote many letters and instructions to Walter, either alone or jointly with the Justiciar Philip Basset or the Treasurer John de Caux (or Caleto), illustrating how efficiently the affairs of England were delegated to his trusted senior servants while he travelled in his French dominions.[29]

In the period 1262-1264, apart from his official duties, Walter was busy on his greatest achievement, the establishment of Merton College. In view of its importance we will describe this development in a separate chapter.[30]

In July 1263 there was a letter to Walter from Bishop Cantilupe of Worcester urging him to persuade the King to accept the terms of settlement proposed by the barons.[31] This seemed to have produced a brief cessation of hostilities. However, later in the year the pendulum swung back again. In July 1263 Walter was ousted from the Chancellorship by Nicolas of Ely, who was appointed for the period of the King's absence abroad. Simon de Montfort marched on London under arms and systematic attacks were made on property belonging to the

King's men. Walter was badly affected. His estates at Malden, Chessington, Farleigh and Cuddington were occupied and stripped in the period June-August 1263.[32] Damage amounting to £ 102 was caused, and it was some years before Walter obtained compensation, although he did quite quickly obtain orders that the occupied properties be returned to him.

In January 1264 Henry III went to France to enlist the help of Louis IX, Walter being appointed with Sir William Latymer to put the King's case in the arbitration.[33] His advocacy was successful but Louis' award, favouring the King, was rejected by the baronial party. Henry returned to raise his army and civil war became imminent. Walter appears to have accompanied him during this time.

In this year the baronial party again moved against the property of the King's supporters. Walter's estates at Malden and Farleigh were once more occupied in March 1264, and some goods were removed (the loss was estimated at £ 42), but more serious damage was done to his prebendal estate at Finsbury, outside the City to the north, estimated at £ 152. In the summer of 1264, now without official employment, Walter obtained orders from the baronial council to recover his estates at Finsbury, Malden and Farleigh [34], and to ensure his personal protection while residing at one of his benefices and while travelling during a defined period.[32] This seems to confirm that the baronial party had no personal quarrel with the King's servants.

The final swing of the pendulum came in 1265, when the King's party triumphed at the battle of Evesham in September. Shortly afterwards Walter appears to have been acting as Archdeacon of Bath, a post to which he had been appointed in 1259/60. The King granted Walter, by way of compensation for the damage done to his property, land up to a value of £ 100, such grant to be satisfied by transfer of (i) land of Robert FitzNigell (ii) land of Gilbert Ellsefeld (iii) London houses belonging to Michael Tony, Stephen Bokerell and William Kane.[36] In addition, to compensate Walter for damage done to his London prebendal property the King granted him a life interest in a moor known as "La More" outside the City walls to the north (probably in the area now known as Moorfields, north of the intersection of the modern streets London Wall and Moorgate).[37] La More had been forfeited by the City of London because of its action against the King's men.

A few years later (1268-71) what appears to be further compensation came to Walter and/or Merton College. Supporters of Simon de Montfort, presumably under pressure from the King, made over property - it would seem on favourable terms.[38] This comprised the Ponteland advowson (transferred by the younger Peter de Montfort) and the estates of Kibworth (Saer Harcourt), Diddington

(St. Maur) and Cuxham, Ibstone and Middleton Cheney (all transferred by Stephen Chenduyt).

After Evesham the King appointed Walter Giffard as Chancellor (and as Archbishop of York in 1266) but employed Walter on a variety of important official assignments over the next seven years.

In 1266 Henry III appointed Walter to inquire into a claim by the nuns of Shaftesbury to a right of wreck based on their fee at Kingston in Dorset (either in the Isle of Purbeck or near Dorchester).[39]

In 1267 the King granted Walter a commission of oyer and terminer (as a travelling Royal judge) to hear complaints by the citizens of Lincoln.[40] Walter also carried out work for the King's brother Richard at around this time. He was one of the three attorneys whom Richard appointed during his absence abroad in 1268.[41]

In 1269 the King appointed Walter and three others as special justices, and in the same year he acted as a judge in the special court of the exchequer of the Jews - a jurisdiction with which, as we have already noted, Walter was particularly familiar.[42]

In 1272 Walter received three special assignments from the King - first, to adjudicate on a dispute in Somerset [43]; secondly, with two others to investigate the activities of some Flemish wool merchants [44]; and, thirdly, a commission of oyer and terminer with three others (including Robert Burnell) to inquire into a dispute in Bury St. Edmunds.[45]

Walter's Household

In 1269 the King granted Walter a further favour. Back in 1264 he had granted him the right to take one or two deer from the Royal forests when travelling on business about the Kingdom. Now this privilege was extended to Walter's valets (or men-at-arms or yeomen i.e. companions rather than servants), and this grant involved listing these men, giving us an opportunity to take an overview of his "familia" or "household", in the sense of his personal staff, similar to the "family" of a general officer in the Army or the "cabinet" of a politician.[46]

The beneficiaries of the 1269 grant were:-

Walter himself
Master Thomas of Bath - Walter's senior clerk, archdeacon of Bath

Thomas Tayllard - second husband of Walter's sister Edith
Roger Tayllard - brother to Thomas
John Wylye - son of Walter's sister Matilda I
John de Basinges - possibly a kinsman of Walter
Hugo Wylye - son of Walter's sister Matilda I
William Wylye - ditto
Nicholas Thedden - son-in-law of Walter's sister Cristina

When Walter became Bishop of Rochester in 1274 he had in addition two principal officials (William St. Quentin and Andrew Kilkenny), two chaplains, a keeper of the wardrobe/ treasurer, and two other officials; on the domestic side two marshals of the horses, three pages, a brewer, a tailor, two cooks, a palfreyman, and three carters. It is conjectured, from the terms of Walter's will, that there were a further 16 servants, giving a total of around 36 in addition to the valets.

Apart from his household, Walter had an extensive "network" of friends, acquaintances, fellow public servants and the like, spread across England, with whom he collaborated on both official duties and private business. In particular, where private interests were involved, it looks as though there were many mutual arrangements, designed above all to save travelling, under which on behalf of each other they negotiated deals, collected and accounted for money and produce, witnessed transactions, pursued legal business &c.   It is interesting to note that after setting up Merton College and transferring its endowments Walter - through his network - continued to manage some of these properties, and by the time of his death had in hand, on behalf of the College, the enormous sum of £ 800 (around £ 800,000 to-day) for which his estate had to account. This ad hoc unofficial national organisation was of inestimable value to Walter's private business, to his charitable and family interests and to his royal patron.

Henry III died in November 1272 at which time Lord Edward, now to be Edward I, was still abroad on Crusade. Despite the absence of the heir to the throne the transition was smooth and peaceful - reflecting a comparatively successful reunification of the kingdom following the baronial troubles. The King's Council appointed Walter once more as Chancellor, probably by pre-arrangement with the new King.[47]   Edward I travelled back in a leisurely way, visiting the Pope and conducting business in France, and landed in England in August 1274. He was crowned at Westminster on 17th. August aged 35.

From 1272-1274 Walter was, thus, effectively Regent of England and was recognised as such, conducting official business as Chancellor, coordinating the activities of the magnates and in touch by letter with Edward I. By a letter of 9th.August 1273 the King thanked Walter for his loyal service and undertook to support his decisions.[48] The uneventful nature of these two years confirms

Walter as truly "a safe pair of hands".

Walter appears to have resigned the Chancellorship as soon as Edward I reached England, since in the 1274 Statutes of Merton College, issued in August of that year, he describes himself as "quondam Cancellarius" - previously Chancellor. He did not, however, describe himself as Bishop-elect, which by then he was.

Walter was elected Bishop of Rochester in July 1274 at around the age of 74.

The Foundation of Merton College (1262-1274)

Walter's most lasting memorial deserves a chapter to itself. We have already noted Walter's lifelong devotion to his extended family and it seems that, as part of it, he had for a long time resolved to provide higher educational assistance for his male collateral descendants. While they were to be the primary beneficiaries, it seems clear from the fact that Walter established a foundation and not simply a fund, that his objectives were both broader and longer-term. Thus to the kin were added other promising young men, initially from the Winchester diocese and, later, from elsewhere as well.

Again, it seems that Walter had for some time (perhaps dating, as discussed in chapter 6, from his secondment to Durham) wished to encourage the provision of well-trained and well-educated young clerks to raise the standard of the secular clergy. He had been educated and trained in an Augustinian house and in the course of his professional career dealt with all the religious orders, so that he fully understood the strengths and weaknesses of these institutions. Further, he had observed - probably, as we have noted, at first hand - the dynamic success of the friars in the universities. Walter's desire to upgrade the secular clergy is not spelt out in the formal Statutes governing the College's activities (although it is perhaps implicit in the subjects to be studied and to be avoided), but it is clearly understood by some of the benefactors of the College and by later commentators on the success achieved by the College in pursuing this objective.[1]

Walter combined his personal, spiritual and intellectual objectives with his long experience of pragmatic management to produce a new type of educational institution, which has been widely copied and adapted both in England and throughout the English-speaking World.

The unsettled state of England in the 1260s, a technical quirk of conveyancing (the need to obtain the permission of the superior lord, being of full age, to the transfer of property as an educational endowment), a characteristic desire to provide for all contingencies and then constantly to review, modify and extend his earlier directions, combined to extend the period of gestation for the foundation from 1262 to 1274. This delay has in the event proved to be an advantage, since by 1274 the College had a definitive constitution which has stood the test of time and attracted many imitators. It was fortunate, too, that Walter, despite his other public duties, remained in good health and available throughout this period to polish and perfect his ideas.

1262 - A False Start

In May 1262 Walter transferred his manors of Malden with Chessington and Farleigh to Merton Priory in trust to provide financial support for clerks studying in the schools in accordance with an ordinance to be executed later. The superior lord of the manors, Richard de Clare, Earl of Clare, Gloucester and Hertford, confirmed the transaction with an imposing list of witnesses, including three bishops, the Justiciar and three judges. It appears that either no ordinance was ever executed or that, while an ordinance was drawn up, it was not fully valid, but it seems that the parties acted as if a valid ordinance was in place, with the income from the manors being made available to Merton Priory. The problem seems to have been that Earl Richard died suddenly in July 1262, so that his heir would have to approve and confirm the overall transfer transaction - but as the heir was then only 19 this could not happen until September 1264.[2]

The fact that the 1264 transfer of the manors took place in a carefully planned series of legal steps only a week or so after the heir Earl Gilbert turned 21 confirms that the sudden death of his father had been the stumbling block.

It has been suggested that the 1262 transfer was a defensive measure by Walter to protect the proposed endowments against his political enemies - the baronial party. If so, it was frustrated by the premature death of Earl Richard, which prevented Walter passing legal possession to the Priory. As already noted, the baronial supporters ravaged the manors in the following year 1263 when Walter was still in possession.

There is no doubt that Walter was a consummate land lawyer and conveyancer and the failure of the 1262 initiative could only be due to something beyond his control - it seems to have been Earl Richard's death when only part of the transaction had been completed. The most interesting distinction between the 1262 transfer and that of 1264 was that the former set up a trust, with Merton Priory as trustee, while in 1264 the transferee was the incorporated College itself. This was the outstanding innovative feature of Walter's imagination - the College was to be free-standing, fully endowed and self-governing, with the only outside influence vested in the "visitor" (the "patronus", initially named as the Bishop of Winchester, but eventually established as the Archbishop of Canterbury)

1264 - The Foundation Effected [3]

The new documentation was executed in August/September 1264. First, Earl Gilbert, the superior lord, gave his consent within a week of coming of age in September. Next, Walter assigned his manors of Malden, Chessington and Farleigh to support his eight named nephews[4], and others up to the number of 20 provided for in the Statutes, while studying in the schools. On 14th.September the representatives of the College took possession; and, finally, on 21st.October the Bishop of Winchester approved the appropriation of the Malden and Farleigh churches to the new House of the Scholars of Merton.

The 1264 Statutes for the Foundation provided for the following:-

- A college of a warden and two or three priests at Malden to administer the manors of Malden and Farleigh to support 20 scholars in the schools at Oxford or at some other seat of learning.
- The scholars to be drawn from the Founder's kin and, to make up the numbers, others, preferably from the Winchester diocese.
- The house to be called the House of the Scholars of Merton.
- The patron to be the Bishop of Winchester.
- Each year on 14th.September 8 out of the 10 scholars were to conduct an inquiry into the management of the house by the Warden.
- A number of administrative matters e.g. the appointment of the students and their allowances; an increase in the number of students if the income rose, so that the existing members could not unduly increase their allowances; special arrangements for orphans and younger boys among Walter's kin (the "parvuli"); expulsion for bad behaviour or for joining a religious order; the election of a new warden; arrangements for sick and incapable scholars and servants.
- Scholars who prospered in life were enjoined to remember their gratitude to the College.

The Statutes were enrolled on the charter rolls - an exceptional arrangement as they normally contained only Royal charters. The first warden was Master Peter Abingdon, a long-standing intimate of Walter. He had been a benefactor and also the second Master of the Basingstoke Hospital. He was an Oxford graduate. By the codicil executed just before his death Walter appointed Peter as chief auditor of his estate.

It looks as though day-to-day operations under the 1264 Foundation continued what had been happening on an informal or unofficial basis since 1262. The young boys and orphans (the "parvuli") stayed at Malden under the eye of the Founder, who appears to have used his Malden manor house as his administrative headquarters [5]: the "older" scholars (some no doubt only in their teens) were in Oxford. Nothing is known about their original accommodation, but by 1266 some at least of the Oxford scholars were living in Bull Hall, off St. Aldates.

Since expulsion is prescribed for Merton students who join a religious order it has been suggested that Walter disliked or disapproved of these institutions. The truth, however, appears to be that he considered it was more appropriate to structure the new "college" for the secular clergy. Walter was himself trained in a religious house and worked with others throughout his life: in addition, by his will he left legacies to eight religious houses with which he had been on friendly terms.

Acquiring the Site 1266-68

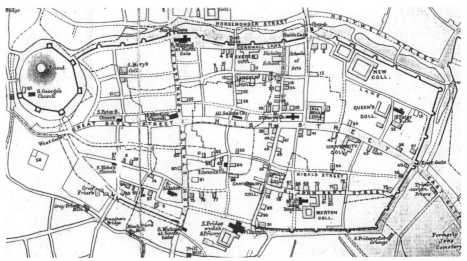

Mediaeval Oxford City and University

Soon after the 1264 Foundation Walter began to buy properties in Oxford to provide a suitable site for the College. His choice of area no doubt depended on availability, and turned out to be in the South East corner of the city, between St. John's Lane (now Merton Street) and the City Wall. The area consisted of a large number of small plots - something that is difficult to imagine to-day with Merton sweeping without interruption from Corpus to Rose Lane - so that patient, piecemeal acquisition was involved. As with all such property developments the pace must be carefully controlled so that the objective - a large area - is attained in an orderly manner. It is hardly surprising that the first conveyances did not appear until January 1266: the completions then continued until Autumn 1268, by which time an acre had been put together.[6].

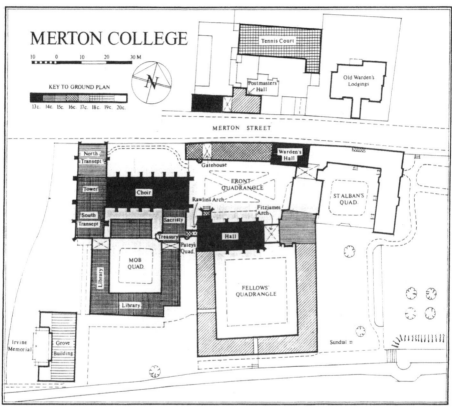

Merton College Buildings

This area included the existing church of St. John the Baptist and its churchyard (The church was sited between the north side of Mob Quad and the College Chapel) and three houses fronting Merton Street - Herprut's House, given by the Priory of St. Frideswide "at the instance of the King" (and subsequently rebuilt as the College's gatehouse), Halegod's House (bought from Jacob the Jew, with the Bek brothers as "sitting tenants") and and Flixthorp's House (adapted around 1270 to provide the Warden's lodging). In 1270-1 Walter acquired property in St. Aldates from Jacob the Jew who had owned Halegod's House in Merton Street.

Merton College in 1621

In 1266 the King gave permission for the enclosure of the one acre site (though the right of access to the City Wall in time of war was preserved) [7]; and in 1267 the King authorised the construction of a watercourse to supply water to the College.[8] It was to run from the River Cherwell, north of Holywell Church, via the Rose Lane area to the College, apparently passing under the City wall. A further royal favour to Walter in 1268 ("my beloved companion") was a year's freedom from tolls on the River Thames for wood, grain and hay.[9] We have already noted the valuable gifts of oak made by the King for the construction of the new College buildings.

Following the acquisition of the core properties, it appears that the College made use of the existing buildings, particularly the three substantial house fronting Merton Street - Herprut's, Halegod's and Flixthorpe's - though the Warden, initially, continued to be based at Malden. The existing church of St.John the Baptist doubled as the College chapel. Actual building (or at least definite plans for new buildings) seems to date from around 1268 with the Royal gift to Walter - already noted - of 8 oak trees "for building the houses of the scholars…and his church at Oxford".

Around 1270 the Warden and the management of the College moved from Malden to Oxford and Flixthorpe's House was adapted as the Warden's lodging. Properties opposite the College on the north side of Merton Street were acquired from the early 1270s.

The Hall was commenced by 1270 and was in use before 1277. Around 1286 Herprut's House was re-built as the gatehouse; in 1288-91 the Muniment Room was built and a start made on the new Chapel in 1290.

While acquiring the core site and preparing plans for building Walter was also organising the investments which would finance the new College.

Marshalling the Endowment (1262-77)

We have already seen that the original endowment (in 1262-4) consisted of the manors of Malden with Chessington and Farleigh in Surrey. Walter now deployed the extensive property portfolio which he had been accumulating and the generosity of the royal family and other benefactors. The unprecedented scale and value of this operation can only be illustrated by listing the estates and advowsons (summarised from ERM)[10]: the dates indicate when they were transferred to the College, and all were paid for by Walter except where otherwise indicated:-

A. Land

1. 1265. Lands belonging to Robert Fitz Nigell (his son married a niece of Walter's) and Gilbert Ellsefeld (described as "enemies and rebels")
2. 1266. The manor of Holywell, outside the Oxford City wall
3. 1268. Land at Seaton Carew, Co.Durham
4. 1268-9. Land at Diddington, Hunts.
5. 1268. The manor of Thorncroft, Leatherhead, Surrey. Given by Philip Basset and Ela, Countess of Warwick.
6. 1268. The manor of Gamlingay, Cambs.
7. 1270. The manor of Stillington, Co.Durham.
8. 1270. The manor of the Dunnings in Cambridge with the so-called "School of Pythagoras" (the ancient stone manor house) and attached lands.
9. 1270. The manor of Ibstone, Bucks.
10. 1270. The manor of Cheddington, Bucks.
11. c.1270. Land at Grantchester, Cambs.
12. c.1270. A half interest in Holywell Mill, given by Osney Abbey.
13. 1271. The manor of Cuxham, Oxfordshire.
14. 1271. Half a knight's fee at Barkby, Leics.

B. Advowsons

1. 1262-64. Farleigh, Surrey.
2. 1264. Malden, Surrey.
3. 1266. St.John the Baptist, Oxford.
4. 1266. St.Peter-in-the-East, Oxford, with the chapels of St.Cross, Holywell and Wolvercote. Given by Henry III.
5. 1266. Wolford, Warwicks. with Burmington. Given by the Priory of Stone, Staffs.
6. 1267. Elham, Kent. Given to the College by the Lord Edward (later Edward I).
7. 1268. Ponteland, Nothumberland.
8. 1268. Half interest in Gamlingay, Cambs.
9. 1268. Diddington, Hunts
10. 1268. Lapworth, Warwicks.
11. 1268. Horspath, Oxfordshire. Given by Richard, Earl of Cornwall and King of the Romans (brother to Henry III)
12. 1269. Stratton St.Margaret, Wilts.
13. 1270. Cheddington, Bucks.
14. 1270. Ibstone, Bucks.
15. 1271. Cuxham, Oxfordshire.
16. 1275. Embleton, Northumberland with the chapels of Rock and Rennington. Given by Edmund, Earl of Lancaster (son of Henry III).
17. 1277. Kibworth Harcourt, Leics.

The Dunnings' Manor House, now part of St.John's College, Cambridge

The three main benefactors of the College (apart from Walter himself) were commemorated in a section of the East window to the Chapel in the 1290s. The arms of Henry III, Edward I (as the Lord Edward) and the de Clare family are displayed in part of the rose at the centre of the window. It will be recalled that Gilbert de Clare, Earl of Clare, Gloucester and Hertford (like his father Richard before him) was the superior feudal lord of the manors of Malden with Chessington and Farleigh and gave his consent to their transfer by Walter to support the new Merton College in 1262 and 1264.

From the East Window of Merton Chapel

Statues of King Henry III and Walter, as the joint progenitors of the College, figure on the Gateway, and it is thought that the busts on the corbels (or label stops) on either side of the east Window of the Chapel (and beneath the arches of the crossing) also represent them, although these carvings are sometimes described merely as of "a king" and "a bishop".[11]

Corbel Portrait of a Bishop, Merton Chapel

The de Clare family was illegitimately descended from the Dukes of Normandy and were prominent in English history both in their own right and by marriage. The name "de Clare" comes from one of their manors, Clare in Suffolk. Their arms were "Or, three chevronels gules" that is, on a gold ground three inverted red chevrons. These arms were "adopted" by the College and, posthumously as it appears, by Walter; but after having been "differenced" - the chevrons instead of being all red, alternated between blue and red.

Walter, being humbly born, was not himself "armigerous" i.e.entitled to bear arms, and there is no record of him having been awarded any, but in due course he used ex officio the arms of the Bishopric of Rochester. It does not appear that he himself ever assumed the de Clare arms, whether "differenced" or not: it looks as though others attributed them to him, probably by "back transfer" from his role as Founder of Merton College, for example on the Gatehouse of the College, on his tomb in Rochester Cathedral and his portrait in the Bodleian (and its copy in Merton Hall). For both the College and for Walter the arms of de Clare (differenced) are often shown "impaled with" that is, combined with, the arms of the Bishop of Rochester. Detailed analysis of this highly technical subject has been produced by Mr. Alan Bott in his Merton College, A Short History of the Buildings 1993; in an article in the Postmaster and The Merton Record, October 1997, and in a definitive work "The Heraldry of Merton College", published in 2001.

While not armigerous Walter had a personal seal and when he became Bishop of Rochester in 1274 he acquired an official seal as Bishop. Initially after the Conquest the Anglo-Saxon practice was followed in England of authenticating documents by having the party to it make a cross and write his name, but sealing took over in the twelfth and thirteenth centuries.[12] This development may have been part of the drive by conveyancers to improve the authenticity of documents affecting interests in land, comparable to the legal fiction under which an artificial dispute over the title was settled and the settlement was enrolled in public court records.

Originally, only monarchs, magnates, high officials and corporations had seals, but this spread downwards through society and by the thirteenth century extended to merchants, traders, small landowners &c. The King and other important magnates had, in addition, subsidiary seals (usually called "small seals") which were held, and used on the principal's behalf, by their officials. In general the importance of the owner was reflected in the size and style of the seal. Royal seals were round and large and two-sided, with the monarch shown enthroned on the obverse and on horseback on the reverse.[13] The English bishops had pointed oval seals, normally one-sided, though Walter's aristocratic protégé, Lord Anthony Bek, on becoming Bishop of Durham, adopted a two-sided bishop's seal. Important individuals showed themselves armoured on horseback and this led to the development of heraldic shields as the seal image. (The inverted chevrons of the Clare family, described above, appear to have originated in inverted chevron designs on their seal in the 12th.century). Non-armigerous individuals made up their own device or adapted standard designs.

Walter's personal seal was, as one might expect, of modest design, being round and small, with a stylised figure or possibly a palm tree in the centre and a motto "Qui timet deum faciet bona" (Who fears God will do good - taken from Ecclesiasticus XV.1)[14] - similar forms of this motto are found on other personal seals. He probably acquired it around 1240 since about that time he sealed the charters endowing the Hospital of St. John the Baptist at Basingstoke, and his seal was also attached to a grant of land to the Hospital at about the same date by his associate Thomas le Forester.

An impression of Walter's Seal as the Bishop of Rochester

Walter's seal as Bishop of Rochester followed the usual "pointed oval" shape. The bishop is portrayed (in the impressions, not the matrix) standing, robed, holding his crozier or staff in his left hand and blessing with his right. There are two subsidiary images of bishops' heads on either side, perhaps to emphasise the continuity of the office. The description running round the circumference of the seal reads "Walterus Dei Gracia Roffensis Episcopus".

An intriguing question arises, since the seal was made for the new bishop, presumably in 1274, is it a contemporary portrayal of Walter ? The figure is tall and fills the length of the pointed oval shape of the seal: we know that Walter stood over six feet, but at the same time this was the conventional way of displaying a bishop on his seal. The figure is also slim, which departs from the tradition (discussed further below in chapter 12) that Walter was heavily built. The face is quite full, however, which ties in with the rounded cheeks of the alabaster effigy on his tomb in Rochester cathedral: this, as we shall see, was made in the 16th.century but may have followed the original effigy on the tomb which it replaced and/or the corbel carving of "a bishop" in Merton College chapel.

Walter sealed the 1264 Statutes of Merton College with his personal seal, but he used his Bishop's seal on the final 1274 Statutes.

The 1270 Statutes [15]

These were much longer than the 1264 Statutes, with more detailed administrative provisions, and no doubt reflect experience gained to date and the substantially increased endowment which Walter had transferred to the College (see above)[16]. Some of these properties represented restitution to Walter for the damage caused to his estates in Surrey and Finsbury by the baronial supporters, as previously described. We do not have details as to whether there was an element of gift, or Royal arm-twisting, or reduction in price, in the relevant transactions, but there is little doubt as to the background where the donors or sellers had been prominent "Montfortians". It is to be noted that Walter, in his will, remembered the individuals who, willingly or otherwise, had compensated Walter and benefited the College. These transactions, completed in what appears to have been a friendly manner, underline the success of the settlement - coordinated by the Papal Legate - which ended the period of baronial unrest and healed the wounds of civil war.

While the "headquarters" of the College are still at Malden, and the scholars are still to be supported at Oxford or elsewhere, the enlarged scale of operations brings an increase in the number of priests, the appointment of two sub-wardens, the appointment of supervisors of studies, and the appointment of land agents ("yconomi") to manage the estates. The Hospital at Basingstoke was confirmed as a refuge for elderly members of the College, and some College income was assigned towards its support.

1274 - The Definitive College Statutes

Walter issued these in mid-1274 when he was relinquishing the Chancellorship and about to take up the see of Rochester. Again, they reflect experience gained and look towards the future when the Founder will have withdrawn, in particular by providing that the warden and 8 or 10 of the senior scholars (effectively "the fellows") may amend the Statutes. This is another example of Walter's prescience, in that the 1274 Statutes - amended by some important parliamentary and Privy Council ordinances - still govern the College to-day.

The College is to be sited exclusively in Oxford. The qualifications, election and duties of the warden are spelled out in detail. The Bishop of Winchester is no longer named as visitor and, in the event, in 1276, he was permanently replaced by the Archbishop of Canterbury. Why was Winchester excluded? Perhaps because the incumbent, Nicholas of Ely, had twice displaced Walter from his Royal employment; or it may simply have been the prestige of having the senior English Archbishop associated with the College.[17]

The financial management of the College was also strengthened. The two sub-wardens were reduced to one but three bursars were to be appointed (from amongst the fellows) who, with the sub-warden and five other fellows, were to oversee the yconomi. The warden was required to visit the estates each year.

The earlier provision that the fellowship should be enlarged if increased income permitted (rather than increasing the stipends) was confirmed. The criteria for recruitment were extended - founder's kin first, then Winchester diocese candidates, thereafter candidates from other dioceses in which the College held land. The number of graduates permitted to study canon and civil law was still restricted to five. Members of the college who prospered in life were again reminded to remember the College and also the Basingstoke Hospital.

The 1274 Statutes were issued in August, with Walter describing himself as "quondam cancellarius", previously Chancellor.

Bishop of Rochester (1274-77)

As we have seen Walter was elected in July 1274, while still Chancellor. He was consecrated on 21st. October in the same year by Archbishop Kilwardby at Gillingham - an unusual arrangement - although he was formally "enthroned" soon afterwards at Rochester. As we commented, earlier, on his appointment as Chancellor, had the times been more peaceful Walter might well have attained a bishopric at an earlier age, perhaps in a more important and richer see, and displayed his proven talents as a dynamic prince of the Church.

It is difficult to escape the feeling that Walter's devotion to Rochester was somewhat half-hearted. While the diocese was small and comparatively poor it was conveniently close to London, Merton/Malden and Oxford - it appears that Walter did indeed want Rochester, as he accepted it while he was still Chancellor [1] - and the accounts we have of Walter for the last three years of his life indicate that he spent much time away from the palace in Rochester.

Rochester Cathedral and Castle from the River Medway

Rochester Cathedral, The West Front

Although Walter did leave two manors to Rochester (Cobhambury, 4 1/2 miles west of Rochester and Middleton Cheney 2 miles north of Banbury in Northamptonshire) there were certainly murmurings in the diocese that he was not as active on behalf of the diocese as he might have been.[2] It is possible that his health was failing at this time. In the spring of 1275 Walter was at Merton Priory, spending much time on writing his will, a long and complicated document. It was witnessed by Archbishop Kilwardby, the Chancellor (successor to Walter), Robert Burnell, the Papal Nuncio and others. Later in the year he is found attempting, unsuccessfully, to purchase for Rochester the manor of Lewisham in Kent from St. Peter's Abbey in Ghent. In the autumn he attended the consecration at Canterbury of Thomas Cantelupe as Bishop of Hereford, and then moved on to Oxford. In 1276 Walter again visited Oxford, attended parliament at Westminster, and at the end of the year followed the Court to Windsor.

In January 1277 he stayed at Halling, an episcopal manor in Kent (some 6 miles south west of Rochester) and visited Oxford in the spring where Merton College had recently (in 1276) undergone a "visitation" by Archbishop Kilwardby: this was Walter's last visit to Oxford and the College. There is some uncertainty about the Archbishop's activity at the College on this occasion. It is generally assumed that he "visited" at Walter's request or at least with his agreement, and that Walter approved of his decisions - even though they represented detailed interference with internal matters - since Walter's seal was attached to the injunctions. The Bishop had not been invited as Visitor (It will be recalled that the 1274 Statutes, unlike the earlier ones, did not specify who the Visitor would be) but he appears to have turned his attention to Merton College in the course of an official visit to the University.[3] The matters tackled would have lent themselves to Walter's management style and meticulous attention to detail. The explanation may be that, since the issue of the 1274 Statutes, Walter considered that it was politic for him to withdraw from any active role in relation to the College - or perhaps, as suggested above, that his health was failing.

He then went on for his last visit to Durham.[4] As was, apparently, the custom for visiting bishops, in order to encourage the major building work that was by then almost finished, Walter issued indulgences to those who visited St. Cuthbert's shrine or contributed to the building cost, and similar indulgences to benefit Finchale Priory. On September 24th. the Bishop of Durham, Robert de Insula, decreed that £ 40 should be paid annually to the Bishop of Rochester in recognition of Walter's special services to the cathedral and see of Durham.

Barely a month later Walter was dead.

Walter's Death

The circumstances and place of Walter's death are not clearly established. The few hard facts are that he died on 27th. October 1277; on the previous day 26th. October he executed quite a complicated codicil to his will, appointed Peter de Abingdon chief auditor of his estate and gave directions about additional gifts and legacies; several identified people were with him i.e. he was travelling with his household; his executors paid Master Martin, a doctor, to attend him at Soleby; and the last definite sighting was at Durham on 25th. September.

Tradition associates his death with a river crossing. One account is that he was drowned while crossing the Medway by boat since there was no bridge [5], but this seems unlikely since he seems to have survived for at least two days. Another speculation is that the accident happened when Walter was fording the Medway at Snodland (some 6 miles south west of Rochester) near the Pilgrims' Way.[6] The most detailed description, however, comes from "the Osney Abbey Chronicler" (Thomas Wykes) - a source which elsewhere in this book (Chapter 12 below) we follow on account of Walter's long and close relationship with Osney, the likelihood that the chronicler himself knew Walter, and the certainty that if he did not some of his colleagues did. In the light of this, the particularity of the description, and the fact that it was contemporary, it is suggested that this must be the preferred version of events.

According to Wykes [7], Walter was travelling through the provinces (peregrando provincias). While there are several possible translations for "provincia" it cannot here refer to the diocese of Rochester, since it is used in the plural. When he was crossing a certain river (fluvium quendam) without particular care (minus provide) by a quite unknown ford (vado prorsus incognito) he was unseated from the horse which he was riding, fell into the river and was with difficulty pulled from the river by his staff. After a short period of time he departed this life.

This account suggests (1) that the accident did not occur in the diocese of Rochester (2) the river was not well known like the Medway (3) the ford was not one with which Walter was familiar.

Turning now to the place of Walter's death, a possible identification of "Soleby" has been with several villages in Kent called Sole Street, in some way associated with Watling Street. However, the match is not close and the suffix -by suggests Danish or Norwegian origins (This suffix is found in Yorkshire and Lincolnshire and adjoining counties, and hardly at all elsewhere)[8], and on the reasoning advanced above we should not be looking near Rochester anyway.

Dr. Highfield has suggested identification with Saleby or Soleby in Lincolnshire, two miles north of Alford.[9] Apart from the exact identification of "Soleby" this location fits better with the leisurely progress of an elderly Bishop, with his entourage, who was last sighted some 200 miles away in Durham around 25th. September, and there was a priory or grange (a subsidiary house) of the Gilbertian order at Saleby, where the Bishop might have been cared for. On the other hand, Saleby is too far away from London for Dr. Martin to have made several visits - something which has been deduced from the wording of the executors' accounts.

The executors' accounts state that they paid "v marc' magistro Martino phisico pro salario suo per multum tempus et pro labore suo de London' usque Soleby ante obitum episcopi". First, the reference to "Soleby", without further description, suggests that it was a quite well known place. Secondly, instead of the traditional translation (many trips from London to Soleby) the entry might be rendered "for arrears of fees over a long period and for his trouble in travelling from London to Soleby before the Bishop's death". If that were accepted Walter would have only have to have survived long enough for word to be sent to London from Lincolnshire and for Dr. Martin to hurry back.

The problem remains, however, that Soleby/Saleby in Lincolnshire is well off any route from Durham to London and Kent, and we know of no reason to take Walter to such a remote area.

An alternative candidate might therefore be considered - Sulby in Northamptonshire, some 6 miles south west of Market Harborough. There is a phonetic fit, and some of the mediaeval spellings of Sulby are close to Soleby e.g. Solebi, Sulehby.[10] Sulby was well-known by reason of a flourishing Premonstratensian Abbey founded in 1155 at nearby Welford and moved to Sulby probably in Henry III's reign. It is much closer to a natural line of travel from the north of England to London and Rochester, and the Abbey was in fact frequently used as a staging post early in the next century by Edward II, particularly on his journeys to and from Scotland.[11] Further, Sulby lies between the estates of Kibworth Harcourt and Middleton Cheney (both natural stopping-off places for Walter), being about 8 miles south of the former and some 26 miles north east of the latter. The distance to summon Dr. Martin from London is also considerably more manageable.

Below the farm which now stands on the site of the abbey there is "a complex system of fishponds and channels connecting with the river Avon".[12] The nearest village is Welford (the original site of the abbey) which may have provided the ford at which Walter's fatal accident occurred.

Walter's Burial and Estate

The Bishop's Tomb [1]

Walter was buried in Rochester cathedral, in the north wall of the north quire transept, in an alcove next to the tomb of St. William (a pious baker from Perth who was murdered near Rochester when on his way to the Holy Land: miracles were reported at his tomb and many pilgrims were attracted, bringing great wealth to Rochester Priory). The tomb was built into the thickness of the wall and windows were opened on the outside to admit daylight. Walter was buried in his Bishop's robes with crozier and chalice.

According to the accounts of Walter's executors the tomb was made in Limoges in France (some 100 miles north east from Bordeaux) and installed at Rochester by the master craftsman John (or Jean), a burgess of Limoges. The total cost of the tomb was over £ 70 or in excess of £ 70,000 in 2000 money.

Limoges work specialised in enamelling metal and, as applied to tombs, appears to have taken two forms (1) in the 12th. Century, a flat enamelled metal slab or plaque positioned on top of the tomb - giving effectively a two-dimensional picture of the deceased (2) in the 13th. Century, a three-dimensional effigy of the deceased formed by covering a core figure made of oak with numerous enamelled copper plates.[2]

It seems likely that Walter's tomb was of the latter type, based on (a) the date (b) a plain flat slab or plaque would be less likely to attract the desecration which subsequently occurred, and (c) the attendance of the master craftsman at Rochester suggests a complicated on-site installation, which would hardly be necessary for fitting a flat slab or plaque.

If that conclusion is valid it seems reasonable to assume that Walter's effigy resembled the only other Limoges tomb recorded in England – that of William de Valence in St. Edmund's shrine in Westminster Abbey constructed in 1296.

(This William was the son of King John's widow by her second husband: he came to Henry III's court in 1247, assumed the title of Earl of Pembroke and served both Henry and Edward I with distinction).

The Tomb of William de Valence, Westminster Abbey

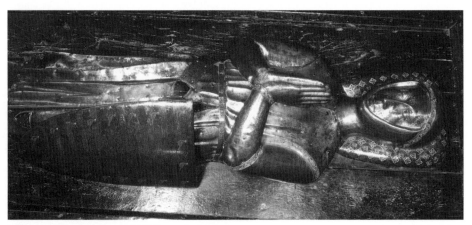

Limoges Work Effigy of William de Valence

William's Limoges effigy has lost much of its enamelling but enough remains to show that this method of enhancing metal could produce a dramatic effect with brilliant colours. The facial features are depicted on a single formed piece of metal, and while somewhat primitive in style, suggest a real person; so we may assume that Walter's effigy also displayed a likeness.

William's effigy is mounted on a plinth or rectangular box (a "tomb box") made of oak and this was also covered with enamelled copper plates which have disappeared. Walter's tomb may have had the same treatment although one reconstruction [4] places his Limoges effigy on a stone slab supported on short metal pillars, a kind of raised table standing on top of the stone coffin. This reconstruction makes a convincing case that the slab which formed this table is the slab which can to-day be seen in the alcove to the left of Walter's tomb.

Slab from Walter's original Tomb, probably the base of the Limoges Work Effigy. (The candle tray added reently)

The question remains, Why did the executors choose a "Limoges tomb" rather than a more usual wooden, stone or metal effigy? In his will Walter did no more than direct the place of his burial, and the executors' accounts simply itemise the work and materials and the costs. Since "Limoges tombs" were French and all the seven executors were English, perhaps the influence of the Papal Nuncio, Roger de Nogeriis - who came from south west France - can be seen: as we note, below, he certainly felt entitled to direct the executors on how to assemble and value the assets of the estate. In any event, as already noted, only one other Limoges tomb has been recorded in England.

Following this uncertain origin Walter's tomb has had a long and complicated history, not all of which has been firmly established. It was damaged during the Reformation in the reign of Edward VI. and Merton College (under the wardenship of Sir Henry Savile) decided to effect repairs - but this turned into a rebuilding operation. In 1598 the tomb was opened, and removal of the slab exposed Walter's remains. The crozier crumbled on being touched but the chalice was undamaged and was removed and taken back to Oxford, probably together with the Bishop's ring. The chalice, according to an account quoted by Bishop Hobhouse, was used at the College as a drinking cup and was later destroyed. He also suggests a possible identification of Walter's ring, stating "A massive gold ring, engraved with a three-quarter figure bearing a palm-branch, and surrounded by a motto "Qui timet Dominum faciet bona" was left by the late Warden Berdmore [1790-1810] to the Compton family and is now worn by the Rev. Berdmore Compton, late fellow of Merton, but of its past history nothing is known. The Founder's signet ring was certainly of this design..."[5] It seems difficult to imagine that a special ring of this kind, carrying the Founder's motto, in the possession of the Warden, can have had no connection with Walter. From the language used it looks as though Bishop Hobhouse had seen the ring and is perhaps seeking to be diplomatic.

More sumptuous ornamentation was added to the tomb and lengthy inscriptions (The main inscription is printed in Appendix III, with an elegant English translation by Mr. Thomas Braun, Dean of Merton College). The Limoges effigy of Walter was replaced by one of alabaster. The windows behind the monument were closed.

The 1598 reconstruction (which was fully recorded in the Merton College register) [6] has given rise to criticism. Bishop Hobhouse in the 19th. Century took Sir Henry Savile to task: "The inscription has little merit.... It seems to deny his chancellorship under Edward I and is calculated to mislead as to the Oxford connection of the college from its first existence, and as to the exact time of the concentration of its detached members, on which point probably Warden Savile was actually misinformed." [7] Several commentators, too, have remarked on the inappropriate clothing of the new alabaster effigy, for example, "It is the figure on the restored tomb that is so interesting. Although the figure is wearing a cope and mitre they are over a rochet and chimere and not of a figure like John of Sheppey [Bishop of Rochester 1333-53, buried near Walter] in full canonicals as it would have been originally. This indicates that when the alabaster figure was made, the sculptor did not have any knowledge of pre-Reformation work or the College authorities did not want it or had forgotten how a mediaeval prelate would have been vested".[8]

In the Civil War the tomb was again damaged ("deformed by rabid fanatics") so the College undertook further repairs in 1662, when Sir Thomas Clayton was Warden.

Another renovation took place in 1701, and in 1770 whitewash was removed from the monument. Its appearance in the 1780s is shown in an engraving published in John Thorpe's Custumale Roffense 1788 during the wardenship of Henry Barton.

By the middle of the nineteenth century the tomb had again deteriorated and the College apparently decided to return it to its original form as described in the accounts of Walter's executors. In 1849, in the presence of Mr. Randolph, the Bursar of Merton College, Mr. Hussey, the architect to the College, and Dr. Edward Hawkins, Canon of Rochester and Provost of Oriel College, the alabaster effigy was moved, the broken slab was lifted and the skeleton was again uncovered.[9] On measurement the skeleton was found to be, in its position in the coffin, exactly 6 feet long. Some traces of the crozier were seen and some small pieces of material, the remains of the episcopal robes. A new slab was installed (the old, broken one appears to be propped up in the next-door alcove to the left of the tomb -

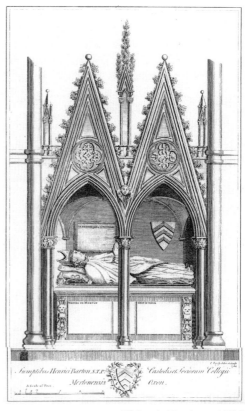

Walter's Tomb in 1788

although, as mentioned above, it has been convincingly argued that this was the "raised table slab" on which the original Limoges effigy was mounted). The alabaster effigy of 1598 was moved to the alcove to the left of Walter's tomb. The windows behind the tomb were re-opened and glazed with stained glass. A simple brass plaque was installed.

The 1849 Plaque on Walter's Tomb

Walter's Tomb Today

Provost Hawkins made a report of these proceedings to the then Warden of Merton, Robert Bullock Marsham.[10] He commented on the earlier removal of the chalice, which was supposed to have been used as a drinking cup at Merton College during the Civil War and to have been subsequently destroyed or lost. Provost Hawkins reported that there was no trace of the Bishop's ring. As mentioned above, there is some evidence that the ring was removed, along with the chalice, in 1598.

Provost Hawkins also expressed the view [11] that, despite the intention, the 1849 restoration would not really make the tomb like the original 1277 work, since "the art is lost". He assigned the alabaster effigy to 1662, rather than 1598.

At some later date, probably early in the twentieth century, the alabaster effigy was placed back upon the slab where it now rests, and the original iron railings were rescued from the crypt of the cathedral and re-installed.[12]

The foregoing - which attempts to harmonise the numerous accounts of the tomb's history - is not universally accepted. For example, Pevsner (Buildings of England, Kent) states " The alabaster effigy is wholly new, designed in 1852 by R.C. Hussey." Another intriguing aspect will strike anyone viewing the effigy without any preconceptions. The feet seem too small for the body, they appear to be of a different material - stone rather than alabaster - and the shoes are

The 1598 Alabaster Effigy of Walter

carefully carved with raised toes and heels in a somewhat different style from the body.

While perhaps technically incorrect, the plain clothing of Walter's effigy, combined with the soft light falling on the alabaster, enhances the impact of the sculpture, giving it a "modern," even timeless, quality: we see a strong but simple man.

The portrayal of Walter's features also deserves consideration. Since the general view is that the alabaster effigy (assigned to around 1600) replaced the original Limoges figure we may hope that it bears some resemblance to the man himself - it is probably the best visual link that we have.

It is noteworthy that Walter, with his meticulous attention to detail, left no direction in his will as to the style of his burial or as to any monument - simply requesting that if he died in Hampshire (which the wording suggests he might have preferred) he should be buried in St. Michael's Church at Basingstoke with his parents, otherwise in Rochester Cathedral. Here, too, we may see Walter's characteristic modesty.

Walter's Will and Estate [13]

Walter died in October 1277 and it took until May 1283 for the administration of the estate to be completed. Considering the complexity of the will, the geographical spread of the assets and liabilities and the friction between William Ewell (Walter's nephew and the main family beneficiary) and the other executors, this was good progress.

The executors had to complete the following steps. On the instructions of the Papal Nuncio they made 20 lists or inventories of personal property in the presence of reliable witnesses in various locations - London (including the New Temple "bank/safe deposit"), Rochester (there were nine separate inventories covering the diocese), Norfolk, Suffolk, Leicestershire, Northamptonshire, Buckinghamshire, Basingstoke, Wiltshire and Dorset. They received claims against the estate and had to sort out disputes, some involving litigation. They sought to recover monies due to the estate. They discharged extensive administration charges in the Royal offices and courts. They had to obtain and pay for legal and other advice. They paid the legacies. And throughout they had to find the cash to pay their own expenses while working and travelling around the country. It was a major operation. The value of the assets which passed through their hands exceeded £ 5,000 (£ 5 million to-day) and of this around £ 1000 represented costs and expenses, indicating the scale and complexity of the task.

The contents of the will illustrate Walter's meticulous style and also his life-long devotion to his family, friends and colleagues, and to institutions with whom he had been associated, including their employees, some in very humble positions. Apart from the customary legacies e.g. to the King, and to his successor at Rochester, Walter left money bequests to

- the poor of ten parishes where he had held livings or prebends
- eight religious houses
- 21 of his kin
- 58 friends, dependants and domestic servants (including the previous owners of estates who had been persuaded to part with their property as compensation for the damage done to Walter's property during the baronial troubles)
- 68 carters and ploughmen in the manors in which he had had an interest.

The legacies to the eight religious houses deserve a comment. They confirm the point already made (when describing the Merton College Statutes which prescribe expulsion for a student who joins a religious order) - that Walter had no prejudice against them: for his new College he simply preferred to exclude monks and friars.

In addition, Walter left valuable chattels e.g. rings, cups, mazers, to nine individuals, and directed that the missal belonging to the Abbot of Osney should be returned to him. To Basingstoke Hospital he left 450 marks (£ 300) to buy land (this was effected in 1283-4) and 100 marks for a chaplain in perpetuity.

Finally, under the terms of the codicil executed on the day before he died, the residue of the estate went to Merton College, possibly to offset the substantial sum of £ 800 which Walter owed to it in respect of rents which he or his staff had collected on its behalf; together with a money legacy of 1000 marks (£ 667, or some £ 700,000 in 2000 money) to buy more land.

Walter's Wealth

For anyone not familiar with thirteenth century English history it is not easy to relate the events of Walter's life to present-day conditions, and in particular the scale of his property "wheeling and dealing". So many customs and conventions were different - for example, the accumulation of a vast fortune by a public servant taking advantage of his position was then fully accepted, to-day it would be regarded as the height of corruption; to have the Pope's representative organise the general settlement of the country after a civil war (incidentally, a brilliant achievement) was accepted as quite natural; close friendship, resulting from years of fruitful cooperation based on complete mutual trust, between the King and his senior officials, who were often of humble origin, was also fully accepted. Again, it is difficult to absorb the idea of the premier public servant, the King's Chancellor, speculating in property and then pouring millions of pounds of his own money (plus contributions from the royal family and other magnates) into a new college, founded to provide education for his kinsmen and to raise the standard of the secular clergy.

It is thought that one way of sharpening the focus would be to relate thirteenth century money values to those of to-day, and put Walter's earnings and investments into a clearer perspective. For a straight conversion of thirteenth century values to those of 2000 we use a multiplier of 1000 x. This is loosely based on the comparison made by the historian D.M. Stenton between the 12th. Century and the early 20th. Century, combined with the UK Cost of Living and similar indices which, conveniently, originated in 1914.[1]

Apart from the Basingstoke family property which Walter inherited and handed over to the Basingstoke Hospital (whence it found its way, eventually, to the College), his wealth came from his stipends and perquisites as a public officer, his church benefices and his entrepreneurial property transactions. Leaving aside his personal expenditure - which appears to have been comparatively modest for his rank and responsibilities - almost all his wealth went into

> - marriage settlements and land transfers for his sisters and their families
> - land and advowsons for Basingstoke Hospital and Merton College
> - legacies under his will.
> - the two estates, Cobhambury and Middleton Cheney, which Walter left to Rochester.

With this approach - looking at the value of the assets acquired rather where the money came from - we can derive an "of the order" approximation of Walter's fortune. The estate, consisting of personal property i.e. not interests in land, and valued at the time by the executors, we can convert by applying our multiplier. For agricultural land we can estimate the acreage and apply a 2000 value, say £ 3000 per acre. For non-agricultural property e.g. the houses purchased in Merton Street, we will have to guess. The same applies to the extent and value of the land transferred to the sisters and their families - some facts are available but not the full details.

Accurate valuation of the advowsons - the right to appoint the priest to a Church living - is difficult. Walter acquired advowsons for the College for two reasons, first, because they represented a good investment and could (as explained below) generate valuable income for the College and, secondly, because they provided opportunities for the well-educated post-graduates from Merton to go out into the parishes and, in due course, if they obtained preferment, to raise the standards of the secular clergy. Suppose the College acquires the advowson for a parish which is worth £ 35 per annum. If, say, £ 10 p.a. would be sufficient remuneration to pay a vicar to run the parish there will be an annual "surplus" of £ 25. With the permission of the Church authorities this surplus could be consolidated into the general funds of an institution like Merton College which had acquired the advowson - a process known as "appropriating the rectory". In our example, the College's income would permanently increase by £ 25 p.a. In fact, of the College's 11 1/2 advowsons, two - Farleigh and Diddington - were never appropriated.

Turning now to valuation, we assume that the capital value of the advowson is 10 years' purchase i.e.10 x the annual surplus of £ 25 = £ 250 (around £ 250,000 to-day). In this way, we can guesstimate that the 9 1/2 appropriated advowsons acquired by Walter for the College have a 2000 value of £ 2.375 million.

We can now attempt a summary:-

	2000 £ Million
11 estates aggregating about 7000 acres @ £ 3000	21.000
9½ advowsons @, say, £ 250,000 each	2.375
2 houses in Merton Street @, say, £ 500,000 each	1.000
4 family settlements, aggregating, say, 500 acres @ £ 3,000	1.500
Kibworth Harcourt c.4000 acres @ £ 3000 per acre	12.000
Gross value of Walter's estate £ 5,111 multiplied by 1000	5.111
Endowment of Basingstoke Hospital, say 60 acres @ £ 3000	0.180
Cobhambury and Middleton Cheney, say 500 acres @ £ 3000	1.500
	£44.666

Clearly this is no more than an approximation. We can make some kind of cross check by looking at Walter's income, bearing in mind that his official positions effectively paid for his accommodation and living costs, and that there was no income tax. We have already noticed that, on appointment as Chancellor, he was allotted 400 marks (£ 267) p.a. to pay for his services and the chancery - at least £ 267,000 in 2000 money. He held around 19 benefices, starting with Cuddington in 1233, and building quite rapidly from around the late 1240s - most of which he continued to hold until his appointment to Rochester in 1274. The value of these benefices aggregated at around £ 500 p.a., or £ 500,000 p.a. in 2000 money.

In addition, the estates which Walter had been acquiring since the 1230s must have generated for him an annual return in rents and produce, before he made them over to his sisters, the Hospital and Merton College.

It is impossible to estimate the profits generated by Walter's property deals, but it is invariably the case that a skilful entrepreneur, *with access to ready money*, can acquire heavily encumbered properties (or in modern times joint stock companies) by paying off the mortgagee at less than the face value of his debt (probably in the 13th. Century inflated by high rates of interest - moneylenders' rates *averaged* 43% p.a.), paying the mortgagor a fair value for his depressed equity interest, and ending up with assets exceeding the value of the cash he has had to lay out.

It is not claimed that this calculation is anything more than a "guesstimate". It was therefore something of a shock to read in March 2000 the "Richest of the Rich" catalogue of the wealthiest 200 individuals in Britain since 1066, published by The Sunday Times newspaper, as a development from its annually published "Rich List". Walter figured as the 180th. richest with a fortune *estimated at £ 2.2 billion in 2000 terms.*

The initial shock was, however, somewhat diminished when the approach adopted by the authors of the Richest of the Rich was studied more closely. Faced with the daunting task of comparing wealth over 10 centuries they adopted a methodology which established the individual's wealth at his/her death (or at its peak if earlier) as a percentage of the country's net national income (similar to GDP) at that time, and then applied the percentage to Britain's net national income for 1999 (which was £ 865 billion).

The Richest of the Rich assesses Walter's wealth at his death at £ 10,000 (£ 5,000 land + £ 5,000 personal property), noting that he had bought an estate for his foundations *but excluding it from the calculation.* The £ 10,000 value at death was taken as the definitive figure and applied to the "net national income" in 1277 (apparently £ 3.8 million) to produce a percentage of 0.26%. This was then applied to the 1999 net national income of £ 865 billion.

Our calculations show Walter's net worth on the same basis i.e. *at his death,* as some £ 18,000 the difference being due to a more generous valuation of his real property. (A valuation of £ 2000 per acre instead of £ 3000 would drop the figure to £ 12,000 not far from the Richest of the Rich figure of £ 10,000)

It therefore seems clear that the wide divergence between our 2000 value and that generated by the Richest of the Rich is due to the conversion from, in this case, 1277 to 2000. (Had the Richest of the Rich taken in all, or even part, of Walter's property portfolio, as we have done, the divergence would have been wider still). The worlds of agricultural England in the thirteenth century and of the commercial and financial United Kingdom in 2000 are too far apart to be bridged in this way: the largest single problem is the development of joint stock enterprises and the generous method by which Stock Exchanges value their future income. The methodology of the Richest of the Rich is, at the same time, an ingenious way of ranking the net worth of a large group of individuals over a 1000 year period.

It is interesting to note that, *in respect of the thirteenth century* the Richest of the Rich ranks Walter at the bottom of the list in equal 11th. place. His contemporary John Mansel, King's Clerk and Secretary to Henry III, occupies the 8th. position. Robert Burnell does not figure. *In the list of richest clerics*, Walter is again at the bottom of the table in equal 17th. position, with John Mansel in 12th. position.

However measured, there is no doubt that Walter became extremely wealthy in relation to his contemporaries. However, since he lived quite modestly, and seemed to manage his wealth as a steward or trustee with long-term ends in view, it is best not to describe him as "a rich man" with its connotations of self-indulgence and extravagance.

Walter's Legacy

W e consider here what kind of man Walter was, and then discuss his educational innovations. Finally, we consider what moral or lessons we can draw from Walter's life and work.

Walter the Man

We have some direct evidence of what Walter was like and more can be deduced from what we know about his life and activities. By any account he was an outstanding person with a most unusual combination of characteristics.

His skeleton measured exactly six feet in his coffin in 1849 "but as it did not lie perfectly straight" [1] we may conclude that in life he stood at least 6' 2" or 3", well above the average height in England in the thirteenth century.

As to Walter's appearance, there is the general tradition that he was not only tall but also well-built, if not portly. At the same time he must have been reasonably fit and athletic as he covered many thousands of miles on horseback during his long life.

Next we can consider the following graphic sources (the numbered images are reproduced on the Back Cover):-

(a) The Bodleian portrait by William Sunman, or Sonmans (Image 1)
(b) The copy of (a) in Merton Hall
(c) The statue on the Gatehouse of the College (Image 2)
(d) The representation of Walter in the carving of the History of St. John the Baptist on the Gatehouse (Image 3)

(e) The representations of Walter on the corbels in Merton chapel (Image 5)
(f) The alabaster effigy over Walter's tomb in Rochester cathedral (Image 6)
(g) The description of Walter's skeleton by Edward Hawkins
(h) The representation of Walter on his seal as Bishop of Rochester (Image 4)

(a) and (b) can be of limited help since Sonmans painted the College Founders from imagination, or using his own models, in the late seventeenth century, but he may have picked up the tradition as to build since he paints Walter as a big man.

The only contemporary record is (h), the Bishop's seal, discussed in chapter 8 above. If it is indeed a likeness, rather than a stylised picture of a bishop, it portrays his height and full face but makes him quite slim.

The representations (c) and (d), both fifteenth century (and probably repaired or re-carved), provide support for the characteristic features. In the charming, somewhat primitive treatment of the History of St. John the Baptist the kneeling Walter is a small, stocky figure with a full face and a benevolent expression. The proportions of the full length statue on the right of the Gatehouse are not altogether happy, but the face is certainly full and the nose prominent: the figure is normal, being neither slim nor stout.

The representations (e) from the chapel (of which a plaster cast is displayed in the Queen's Room at the College) are of considerable interest, particularly since they have not been exposed to the weather and so there has been no repair or re-carving. In the chapel on either side of the east window (completed around 1290) there are carved corbels (or label stops). They are sometimes described as being of "a bishop and a king" [2], though usually identified as being of Walter and Henry III, presumably as the joint progenitors of the College. Similar carvings are found in the crossing. There are two (one damaged or removed) at the base of the arch at the west end of the chancel; two at the base of the arch on the north side of the crossing; and one at the base of the arch on the south side of the crossing i.e.at the south east corner of the crossing. The crossing was built later than the east window, around 1330. These carvings are difficult to examine in situ but the plaster cast (which is taken from the carving on the north side of the east window) deserves careful study. Overall the bust has something of a pixy appearance, with protruding ears, prominent lips, displayed open, and a long chin - probably to give a "normal" image when viewed from ground level. The bishop is portrayed as quite young, perhaps around 45, though Walter was probably over 70 when he was appointed to Rochester. He is wearing a "travelling" mitre, shorter in height and made to fold up - perhaps recognising the time that Walter spent travelling during his short reign at Rochester. Did the sculptor, working some 13 years after Walter's death, carve from imagination, or follow contemporary convention (as with the carvings of monsters and green men who also figure in the chapel), or did he use some sketch or portrait of Walter since lost, or did he perhaps visit the Limoges effigy at Rochester? Since he was at the same time carving "the king" (Henry III), who had been dead some 17 years - but of whom there must have been many representations available - it is reasonable to assume that he was indeed striving for a likeness for "the bishop". Leaving aside the age disparity, it is possible to see some resemblance between the corbel plaster cast and the 1598 alabaster effigy at Rochester (considered below), with regard to the fullness of the lips, the vertical creases in the cheeks and the strength of the chin.

The alabaster effigy (f) made around 1600, is the finest portrait, both in quality and materials. It shows a full face with prominent cheeks and a worldly look around the mouth, and its overall expression could be described as strong but kindly, reflecting Walter's main characteristics. It was made to replace the original effigy over the tomb, probably (as discussed above) of wood overlaid with Limoges enamel work, which was damaged in the reign of Edward VI. In terms of a real link with Walter we must assume or hope that enough remained to give the seventeenth century sculptor a feel of the original likeness. As already noted, some resemblance to the corbel carving can be seen, so it is possible that the sculptor had seen the corbels at Merton College.

Regarding (g), Provost Hawkins in 1849 commented, after examining the skull, that Walter had a low forehead and that his eyes were close together [3]. This suggests that he was not conventionally handsome, but might indicate a shrewd, observant expression - again in line with what we might deduce from Walter's practical attitude to life.

Since we are left with little more than a tall, heavily built, imposing man with a strong and worldly but kindly appearance, we could do worse than adopt the image portrayed in the alabaster effigy in Rochester cathedral as our best representation of Walter. Perhaps when the tomb is next opened it will be possible to take an impression of the skull and rebuild the features, as is now frequently done - with considerable accuracy - for genealogical and forensic purposes.

We pass now to Walter's personality and character. The Latin obituary verses quoted by Thomas Wykes, Canon of Osney Abbey ("the Osney Chronicler") are set out in Appendix II together with an elegant English translation by Thomas Braun, Dean of Merton College. Bishop Hobhouse, who reproduced the verses in his Sketch of Walter's Life in 1859, took the view that they were probably composed by Wykes himself, but, if this is not the case, they were evidently written by someone who knew Walter well [4]. We have already noted Walter's long and close connection with Osney Abbey. The warm sentiments expressed are also in line with the comments (see below) which the Chronicler made in 1274 on Walter's appointment as bishop of Rochester.

Dealing first with personal qualities, Walter is described as honest; companionable - perhaps good company or even "clubbable"(socialis); just; chaste (mentioning this quality in a churchman committed to celibacy perhaps suggests that Walter was exceptional in this regard: certainly Walter stressed in powerful terms the dangers presented by women, when he prohibited - in the College Statutes - their employment by the College). Regarding behaviour, Walter was prudent or shrewd in giving advice (cautus consilio); unspoiled by his high position (culmine sincerus); of pleasant bearing; modest in speech (sermone modestus), and hospitable. More general comments about him - of dazzling integrity; of good repute; he loved the clergy; the student body speaks well of him; and Oxford scholarship blooms because of him.

Wykes' comments on Walter's appointment to Rochester in 1274 are equally enthusiastic (again in Mr.Braun's translation) " a bountiful man, fully erudite in secular wisdom: he was ever, by providing for religious men, above everything in his dealings, the readiest helper and patron".

The consistency of these two Osney opinions, and the detail of the verses, go some way to discount obituary distortion or flattery.

A light-hearted poem by a Merton undergraduate in 1934 [5] draws some similar deductions about Walter's personality from the 1598 alabaster effigy at Rochester:-

> *Walter of MERTON, at your splendid shrine*
> *In Rochester cathedral where you lie*
> *I fancy Angel Stewards pouring wine*
> *To pledge that College Founders never die.*

> *How else can I explain that cheerful look*
> *That brightens your stone features like a gem?*
> *"My meeting went according to the book*
> *(It says) and I was far too good for them!"*

> *The timeless essence of well-bred success*
> *That hangs about Bank chairmen clings to you*
> *"Their questions on the accounts I must confess*
> *were ill-conceived and mercifully few !"*

> *AUDITU MALI? - He was never rash.*
> *Bad news is good news if you have the cash!*

We have referred above to Walter's friendship with his patron and sovereign Henry III who frequently referred to him in formal documents as his companion and beloved clerk. On one occasion he spelled out his loyalty to the Crown in a public document: when granting Walter a life interest in La More (the area around Moorfields, north of the City of London) as compensation for the damage done to his prebendal estate at Finsbury, he commented "qui nobis tempore turbacionis predicte fideliter adhesit" (who faithfully supported us in the said troubled times). He was equally trusted by Henry's son Edward I who left England in his charge 1272-4 [6], though, with the age differential, there was obviously not the same personal friendship as with his father. Walter also worked for Richard, Earl of Cornwall and King of the Romans (King Henry's brother) and appears to have been on friendly terms with him [7]. Along similar lines, in 1257 the King wrote to his secretary John Mansel and referred to Walter as "my clerk and a friend and well-wisher of yours" [8], so as fellow servants of the King they must have been on good terms with each other.

It seems very likely that Walter inspired the same warmth of feelings from others in less exalted positions. First, we have three examples derived from property transactions, suggesting, that Walter tended to find deals among those with whom he was on friendly terms, and that he had the rare gift of obtaining good deals for himself while remaining on excellent terms with the other party. William de Hanyton (probably Hannington about 7 miles north west of Basingstoke), who parted with land in favour both of Walter and his brother-in-law Richard Elvet around 1240, refers to him in the transfer as "his beloved companion and friend". The same description was used by Geoffrey des Roches who granted Walter a meadow in c.1235. In 1247 Ralph Amundeville, in granting Walter his manor of Stillington, called him "beloved companion and special friend". While probably taken from "common form" or precedent books these terms of endearment carry some weight - not least because they are not used on every occasion.

We have already noted the observations of the Osney Chronicler - "He loved the clergy" and "The student body speaks well of him".

Some of the provisions in Walter's will underline his ability to be on friendly terms with all conditions of people, for example, on the one hand, his gifts to Lord Anthony Bek (whom he met through the purchase of Halegod's House and whose career he promoted); on the other hand, the legacies to Peter the Cook, Henry the Cook and John the Taylor; to Adam the Palfreyman; to William the Cook at Osney; Geoffrey the Carter, Richard the Carter and Walter the Carter; and finally the portmanteau legacy of 5 shillings (£ 250 in 2000 money) to each of the carters and ploughmen on all his manors - 65 of these legacies were paid. The carters, in particular, were probably well known to Walter as they would have handled the baggage train of his household whenever he visited the manors in question.

Another feature of Walter's friendships was their longevity - a telling indication both of his sincerity and of the irrelevance of Walter's rise to fame and wealth. His friendship and working relationship with Peter de Abingdon must have exceeded 40 years. Walter bought the manor of Malden from the Watevill family in 1240 - he left a legacy to John de Watevile in 1277. The same applied to his purchase from the Waltham family in around 1240 - Robert de Waltham received a legacy in 1277. When Walter was at Durham in the 1240s William of Sedbergh was a colleague and they continue to collaborate when Walter moved back to the south: he, too, received a legacy in 1277. Again, Thomas le Forester worked with Walter from around 1240 and received a legacy in 1277.

Perhaps the most remarkable example of Walter's ability to generate friendship was his relationship with the "Montfortians" who had been involved with damage to Walter's estates in Surrey and London in the time of the troubles. They had plundered his patiently assembled possessions in a civil war situation, challenging the legitimacy of his master Henry III - an action bordering on treason. This was in 1263-4. After the settlement of the baronial troubles - itself a model of civilised behaviour - they made over property to Walter or directly to Merton College later in the 1260s. They can hardly have been pleased either to find themselves on the losing side or to be parting with their heritage to a humbly born career civil servant (though in two or three cases it may have enabled them to escape from the pain and disgrace of being sold up by moneylenders). But the deals were done - and Walter apparently made friends of his master's enemies. Walter then showed considerable kindness and generosity, over a period of time, particularly to the FitzNigells, supporting the marriage of his niece Agnes to Robert FitzNigell junior, providing a dowry for the FitzNigell daughter Matilda and finally, by his will, returning to Robert junior his interest in the FitzNigell land and bequeathing him 130 marks (say £ 87,000 in 2000 money) to restore his property ("ad terras suas instaurandas"). Walter left 80 marks (say £ 50,000 in 2000 currency) to the Chenduyt daughters (Middleton Cheney and neighbouring estates) and a legacy to Saer Harcourt (the Kibworth Harcourt estate). Henry St.Maur (the Cheddington estate) and Peter de Montfort (the Ponteland advowson) did not benefit under Walter's will but were honourably associated with the foundation of Merton College as benefactors.

Walter's pious devotion to his parents and his care for his extended family, implemented in a variety of ways, have been described on a number of occasions. Apart from advancing in life his nephews, nieces and cousins he continued to stand by them after he had risen in the world. For example, when Richard fitz Elyet (probably Richard Oliver, Walter's nephew) was fined 20s. for trespass in 1247, Walter stood surety for him [9]. Again, in 1261 Walter procured a pardon for his nephew Walter, son of Peter de la Clythe who had killed Nicolas le Webbe of Basingstoke: we do not know the circumstances, but obviously a pardon was needed [10].

The greater part of this account of Walter's life has been taken up with describing his professional skills, whether these were being exercised on behalf of his employers or his Royal patron or in pursuit of his private, family or charitable interests. Traditionally conveyancers and property lawyers are considered dry, introverted and rather boring. While undoubtedly patient, meticulous and erudite, Walter was probably something more. He appears to have been brisk and businesslike, extremely energetic and persistent, entrepreneurial - spotting opportunities for a deal or a profit - and at the same time worldly and sociable. Whether engaged on a complicated land deal or an international negotiation he got on with the business in hand and was almost invariably successful.

We can have no direct knowledge of Walter's religious and spiritual feelings. In his formal documents, especially his will and the charter endowing St. John's Hospital at Basingstoke, he gives all the indications of intense piety and devotion. He was a late ordinand but his public duties do not seem to have left him much time for any cure of souls, and as Bishop he was frequently out of his diocese. However, from the style of his life and his constant concern for others we may conclude that, whatever his private beliefs (and we have no reason to think him other than devout and committed) he lived a truly Christian existence.

There are few, if any, reports of criticism or dislike. There were mutterings that Walter did not exert himself enough for Rochester Priory when he was Bishop [11], but we have commented that this may have been due to his other preoccupations or failing health - or perhaps was simply unjustified. In the baronial troubles Walter's properties were ravaged - though he was certainly not the only victim - and he was quickly put back into possession by the baronial party (and, in due course, well compensated), so that the whole affair seems to have been political rather than based on any personal animosity.

All in all, we can, like his contemporaries, only marvel at the complex of characteristics in his personality, the achievements of his life and his unique educational legacy. Our perception of Walter reflects his own philosophy of life, encapsulated in the motto on his personal seal "Qui timet Deum faciet bona" - Who fears God will do good.

Walter - The Educational Pioneer

When Walter founded Merton College in 1262-74 he had, as we have seen, a particular objective in mind even though it is not spelled out in the statutes - to turn out well-educated postgraduates to raise the standards of the secular clergy (in addition to providing higher education for his kinsmen). This influenced a number of the rules laid down, particularly the syllabus to be followed and the limitation on other courses of study. But this did not affect the structure of the new College itself.

There were a number of institutions of higher education already existing both in England and Europe, and a range of religious houses - with which Walter was familiar - whose activities included education. While Walter appears to have drawn on these for a number of aspects of the new College, we concentrate here on what was truly original, since this was his real legacy. As with all successful inventions or innovations, once created they appear to be natural, sensible, almost inevitable - it is just that no one had thought of them before.

These original features were:-

1. Independence.
So long as the Statutes were observed no civil or ecclesiastical authority was to be able to interfere in or direct the affairs of the College. There was to be only the Visitor ("patronus"), originally named as the Bishop of Winchester, but in course of time established as the Archbishop of Canterbury, the English "metropolitan". This appears to have been established by the "visitation" in the last year of Walter life (1276) of Archbishop Robert Kilwardby, who had recently consecrated Walter as Bishop of Rochester. In fact the Archbishop did on that occasion interfere extensively with the internal affairs of the College - innovating as well as correcting - but this seems to have occurred with Walter's concurrence (his seal was attached to the injunctions). The principle of independence, however, did survive.

2. Self-sufficiency.
Walter endowed the College with a huge, unprecedented endowment, primarily from his own resources but also with the contribution of Royal and other benefactors. Other educational establishments depended on "alms" (secured in the "university chest"), specific gifts or a series of subventions, so that the future was always less than secure, and the attention of those in charge was always engaged in fund-raising and maintaining solvency.

While the scale of the endowment was large, Walter was not able to foresee the problems of inflation. On the other hand the College has on occasions benefited from "windfalls" e.g.disposing of farming land for building purposes.

3. The Dual Role of the Warden and Fellows.
While the Statutes direct that the Warden is to be particularly concerned with looking after the assets of the foundation, the Warden and officials of the College are responsible both for managing the College and for managing the endowment. The latter was to be handled on a day-to-day basis by specialists - the yconomi

and bursars (and in later years by land agents, stockbrokers &c.) - but the overall responsibility remained. When one observes the disasters which overtake organisations in which "running the operation" becomes divorced from "finding the money", the wisdom of Walter's arrangements is fully apparent.

4. Negative Definition of the Objective

As already noted, there is no overt reference to the desire to turn out well-educated priests, though the subjects to be studied and to be avoided are spelled out. The Statutes are clear, however, in excluding the distractions from their duty to study which might be found in a religious house. The perpetual obligations of worship and prayer are to be handled on behalf of the College by altar priests appointed for the purpose. The graduate students are not to be engaged in manual work. And, in particular, the support of the College would be withdrawn from any member who undertook religious vows..

5. Self-Policing of the Size of the College

Walter carefully arranged for the College to expand as funds permitted, realising the natural inclination of those in charge of any organisation to feather their own nests at the expense of the underlying objective. This injunction has not always been observed but the built-in checks and balances have ensured that corrective action was taken.

Adaptation and Development

There are many other interesting and ingenious rules and regulations in the College's Statutes - reflecting Walter's long and successful experience of managing people and institutions - but these are incidental, not part of the core design. Within a few years of Walter's death (and Archbishop Peckham's forceful insistence upon the original requirements of the Statutes in 1284) the restrictions on the subjects to be studied were "honoured in the breach" as the College attracted outstanding scholars in medicine, mathematics, physics and astronomy in the first half of the 14th. Century. Change in the subjects being studied has made no impression on the effectiveness of the College structure.

An interesting development in modern times - which might be said to be implicit in Walter's policy of full endowment - is the objective of providing College accommodation for all students. In this the wheel has come full circle since the problems of lodgings "in the Town" were a major factor in the Town and Gown disturbances in the 12th. and 14th. Centuries.

Walter clearly envisaged the development within the College of a family-style loyalty and devotion (so strongly exemplified in himself), particularly in his provision that graduates who prospered in life should remember the College. The family style of relationship inherent in the small to medium sized college (like Merton and all those which consciously or unconsciously imitated it) is a unique result of this, not to be found in monolithic universities lacking constituent colleges. The nearest comparisons in England are probably to be found in the public schools, in livery companies and in Army regiments, where there is also, very often, a lifelong family-style devotion and affection and a "support network" for individuals who encounter problems or fall on hard times. Another, much later, spin-off from the college family model is the tutorial method of instruction. While in public lectures the relationship is between the professor "laying down the law" and the "respectful" students listening, in a tutorial there is (at least in theory and, depending on the calibre of the tutor and the students, even in practice) a measure of discussion and debate on equal terms within the college family. Most students will have several tutors, and there are many stories of life-long enthusiasms being inspired by charismatic tutors.

Following the Model and its Features

As noted above, the College perfected its Statutes over the 1264-74 period. Statutes were adopted by University College in 1280 and by Balliol in 1284. The pattern of the Merton Statutes (the "Regula Mertonensis") was followed, deliberately by Peterhouse, Cambridge and Oriel College, Oxford and effectively by all subsequent English university colleges. The pattern is echoed, too, by the earlier foundations in North America like Harvard (via Emmanuel College, Cambridge), William & Mary, Yale, Princeton, Columbia, Brown and Rutgers, and, in another form, the idea of self-sufficiency is implicit in the system of land-grant colleges across the United States [12].

The originality of Walter's concept, and its success, can hardly be exaggerated.

Conclusions

It is tempting to seek to draw from Walter's educational pioneering some ideas which might be relevant to the current debate on higher education in the UK - but this temptation must be resisted as this book is not the place in which to embark upon such a politicised topic. In any case it may be doubted whether 13th. Century ideas, as such, can have any real relevance to the 21st. Century.

What remains valid, however, from studying the achievements of Walter (and others like him) is the way in which problems and new ventures are approached and tackled - and this is of course not confined to educational or academic matters. These less exciting aspects of "conducting business" are usually the determining factors in whether a good idea is or is not successfully translated into action. Many examples can be drawn from Walter's career, for example:- any important new project needs patient thought, meticulous planning, perhaps some trial and error; the visionary or "ideas man" is not usually the best person to manage the newly established venture; in a set of rules (like the College Statutes) there should be built-in checks and balances and as much "self-policing" as possible, and as little reliance on "outside" enforcement as possible; overall responsibility for an operation covers both "administration" and "managing for profit", and so on. If this discussion is beginning to read like a management manual, it is because this is one of the key elements in Walter's character - his down to earth practical management skill with people and resources. When combined with his intelligence, charm, energy and creativity, it set him apart from almost all his contemporaries, and is probably the main reason for his phenomenal success in the public service.

Clever new ideas are always plentiful: assessing "whether they will work" and converting them into viable products and services requires management skill - and this applies equally to the commercial world and the public sector. This quality Walter undoubtedly had. It is also strongly exemplified in the 19th. Century entrepreneurs (many of whom were engineers) who made sweeping innovations in manufacturing, infrastructural works, canals, railways, shipping, publishing &c. But management skill cannot operate in a vacuum. The 19th. Century innovators had their own money or they found rich private patrons and the backing of joint stock companies; while Walter accumulated great wealth in land holdings and enjoyed the patronage of the King.

Walter's legacy in this area, therefore, is quite simple, if not very glamorous - given the visionary idea and the necessary resources, practical achievements require practical management skills, patience and hard graft.

ABBREVIATIONS

B & M	History of Basingstoke, Baigent & Millard
ChR	Charter Rolls
CMH	Cambridge Mediaeval History
Coates	The Place Names of Hampshire, Richard Coates
CR	Close Rolls
DNB	Dictionary of National Biography
Douie	Life of Archbishop Pecham, D.Douie
ERM	The Early Rolls of Merton College, J.R.L.Highfield
FC	FitzNells Cartulary, Surrey Record Society 1968
Heales	The Records of Merton Priory, A.Heales
HEL	History of English Law, Holdsworth
HILL	Historical Introduction to the Land Law, Holdsworth
HMC	History of Merton College, Martin & Highfield
Le Neve	Fasti Ecclesiae Anglicanae 1066-1300, John Le Neve, ed.Greenway 1971
LQR	Law Quarterly Review
MP	Merton Priory, Museum of London & Merton Borough
P & M	History of English Law, Pollock & Maitland
PR	Patent Rolls
Plucknett	Concise History of the Common Law, T.F.T. Plucknett
Postmaster	Postmaster and The Merton Record
Shore	History of Hampshire, Shore
Sketch	A Sketch of the Life of Walter de Merton, Bishop Hobhouse
Stanley	Within Living Memory, Diana Stanley
Stenton	English Society in the Early Middle Ages, D.M.Stenton
VCH	Victoria County History
Wilks	History of Hampshire, Rev. Theodore Wilks
Willis	Historical Miscellany of Basingstoke, Willis

Notes

Chapter One - Origins

1. His parents lived in the middle of the town, close to the church
2. B & M 359-60
3. Wilks VIII 224n; Coldicott, Hampshire Nunneries 34-7
4. See B & M index of names "Herriard"
5. Ibid. "Cook"
6. The regulations were formally recorded in 1389 but had been in force long before: see B & M 213
7. This was the manor of Basingstoke Merton: see ch. 7.
8. HMC 324n.
9. Stanley ch.3.
10. Ibid., quoting Sarah Portsmouth, niece of Edmund. See Hants & Berks Gazette 12 January 1940.
11. Basingstoke Gazette 5.11.1999. The local historian Mr. Arthur Attwood describes the history of St. John's School.

Chapter Two - Basing & Basingstoke

1. Shore 169; VCH Hampshire IV.129
2. See B & M 64-5
3. The Hampshire Independent 14.12.1889. A review of B & M.
4. See VCH IV.133
5. VCH IV.134.
6. VCH IV.115
7. VCH IV. 126-7
8. Ibid.
9. Heales 29.
10. These are described below. A full listing of the Priory's portfolio c.1242 is in Heales, Appendix LXVI. The Priory had other Hampshire investments, more distant from Basingstoke/Basing, at Winton (Winchester), Alresford, Sutton

(Bishops Sutton), Ropley and Headley (between Alton and Hindhead)

11. ERM 8
12. B & M 382
13 This account is summarised from VCH.IV.42 ff.
14. VCH IV 107
15. VCH III 383

Chapter Three - Early Life and Education

1. ERM 9; Heales 39 2. ERM 10; HMC 6.
3. HEL II 494; LQR January 1891 at 193; P & M. I. 219
4. Plucknett 216 ff.
5. HILL 136
6. HEL III.218-9; LQR Jan.1891 at 199
7. Ibid.
8. The text is in B & M 596
9. Wilks at VIII.224. notes that several of the priors of Merton were natives of North Hampshire e.g. Henry de Basinges 1231-8; Gilbert de Ash (Ashe is a village 7 miles west of Basingstoke) 1263-92; Edmund de Herriard 1296-1305.
10. MP 7
11. The Catholic Herald 4.6.1999
12. This summary is based on CMH VI.585 ff; Powicke, The 13th. Century 256 ff. and Stenton 257-8.
13. Sketch 21
14. This account is derived from Salter's Survey of Oxford 10-13.
15. Heales 41
16. The famous letter is discussed more fully in ERM 9-10

Chapter Four - Merton Priory: The Professional Clerk

1. See ERM 8.
2. See ERM 51-2
3. The relevant deeds are printed in B & M 594 ff.
4. FC lxiii
5. Most of the deeds can be found in B & M 596 ff.and FC documents 27, 42, 52, 54, 56, 58, 60 and 61.
6. Some support for these assumptions (of Walter's involvement) is given by the analysis of the Blanch and Ballard purchases for Agnes and Gilbert Ewell: see FC lxiii.
7. For some clues see FC lix and lxi. Regarding their seniority by age the outline family tree (Appendix I) follows the table of Founder's Kin in Merton College records (see ERM 451) dated to 1320-40. While some known kin are omitted

from the table it is likely to be accurate since admission to the College turned on establishing kinship.
8. Coats 57 "Cliddesden"
9. See FC lix.
10. See B & M 183
11. FC lviii.
12. See ERM 40 and FC lxi ff.
13. Coates 154 "Stakes"
14. Ibid 175 "Wickham"

Chapter Five - Royal Service: The First Phase

1. See ERM 10.
2. CR 11.7.1240
3. A summary is given below: for a fuller analysis see ERM 12-14 and FC lxiii ff.
4. B & M 42; VCH Hampshire II 105, 208
5. The deed is printed in B & M 598
6. Wilks VIII.223n.
7. See B & M 29-30, 31
8. The second deed is printed (in Latin) in B & M 612 and (in English) B & M 44
9. These gifts of land are documented in B & M 593 ff.
10. The last fellow accommodated in the Hospital was Walter Staunton c.1381-1402/3: see HMC 324n.
11. Wilks 226. The VCH Hampshire II 209 is more critical "In 1379 the college began the unhappy principle of leasing the hospital". These leases (from 1379 to 1695) are in B & M 614 ff. The last reference to an inventory of chapel goods was in 1502 and to the maintenance of a chaplain in 1543.
12. See B & M 50-51.
13. See VCH II 210 describing letters written in 1772 and 1773 to the bursar of the College by Thomas Warton, Poet Laureate and Professor of Poetry and Ancient History at Oxford, and son of a famous Vicar of Basingstoke.
14. The 1443-4 Terrier of Hospital lands totals around 278 acres: the 1578 Terrier some 251: B & M 617 ff. This excludes crofts, garden plots &c for which no acreage is given.

Chapter Six - Serving the Prince Bishop

1. Walter's activities at Durham are described in greater detail in ERM 15-18
2. See FC lxviii.
3. See Douie 98 ff. for discussion of the rule and Peckham's efforts to enforce it. The rule, while "in force", had not been promulgated in England.
4. The transaction is described in greater detail in ERM 17

5. By Mr.Alexander Murray of University College, Oxford: see University College Record (2000) XII.4

6. Already suggested in ERM 68

Chapter Seven - Royal Service: The Second Phase

1. See Sketch 4
2. Ibid
3. ERM 18
4. VCH IV 132
5. Ibid
6. Mrs.Anne Hawker, unpublished notes
7. Ch.4 above See also the town plan of Basingstoke at p...above
8. See B & M 70; ChR 8.11.1256
9. Quoted in Willis 32
10. B & M 333, VCH Hampshire IV 134
11. Hants & Berks Gazette 24.1.1936.
12. By fine: see Visitations of Hampshire 1530,1575, 1622-34 published by the Harleian Society 1913, pedigree of Fisher 64-5.
13. See B & M 201
14. The deeds are printed in B & M 606
15. Sketch 5
16. CR May 1255, CR December 1261 17. See CR in the years mentioned.
18. See CR in the years mentioned
19. CR 42 and 43 Henry III; PR 5.6.1259.
20. DNB. "Walter de Merton"
21. PR 15.6.1259; PR 11.1.1263; Le Neve 37,50.
22. CR March 1260
23. PR 13.7.1261
24 PR 11.12.1261
25. PR 20.6.1262
26. PR 11.1.1263
27. Sketch 7
28. PR 22.5.1260; CR 11.5.1260
29. CR passim in 1262
30. See ch.8.
31. Sketch 7
32. For further details see FC lxx-lxxi.
33 PR 5.1.1264
34. CR 9.8.1264
35. PR 48 Henry III m.9, m.7.
36. ChR 24.10.1265. This appears to be the effect: there are gaps in the text.
37. PR October 1265

38. Discussed further in ch.8
39. PR 6.12.1266
40. PR 4.11.1267
41. CR 52 Henry III (1265), PR 8.7.1268
42. Sketch 33
43 PR 23.2.1272.
44. PR 20.2.1272
45. PR 29.10.1272
46. PR 48 H III m.3: CR 18.12.1269
47. CR November 1272: See Sketch 36
48. See Sketch 36

Chapter Eight - The Foundation of Merton College

1. See the authorities quoted in Sketch 23-4
2. The complicated arrangements are analysed in ERM 21-2
3. A fuller account is in ERM 25-7
4. John, William and Roger de la Clythe; Robert and Philip de Ewell; Thomas de Worting; Walter Elvet and Walter de Portsmue.
5. ERM 52
6. See ERM 52 and the documents printed at 403 ff.
7. See ERM 403
8. The text of the document is in ERM 406-7
9. PR 28.3.1268
10. ERM 45-9
11. E.g.Royal Commision on Historical Monuments, City of Oxford 78
12. See Encyclopaedia Britannica "Seals"
13. Ibid.
14. I am indebted to Mr. Thomas Braun for this reference
15. The full text is in ERM 378 ff.
16. There is a listing of the properties transferred to the College in para 33 of the Statutes
17. This seems to have been the view of Archbishop Peckham: see HMC 46-7

Chapter Nine - Bishop of Rochester

1. ERM 30
2. According to the Rochester Chronicler, Haddenham: see ERM 30. The mutterings were strongly criticised in Custumale Roffense 192
3. The visit is fully discussed in HMC 46 ff.
4. A more detailed account is in ERM 32-3
5. Kilburn, Survey of Kent 228

6. Archeologica Cantana LVIII 1974 "The Medway Crossings of the Pilgrims' Way"

7. Chronicon Thos. Wykes 107

8. See P.H. Reany, English Place Names 171

9. ERM 33

10. Northampton Central Library, Local Studies Librarian; Mawer & Stenton, Place Names of Northamptonshire

11. VCH Northamptonshire 138 at 139

12. A Guide to the Abbeys of England and Wales, Anthony New 368-9

Chapter Ten - Walter's Burial and Estate

1. This account has drawn on the following: Custumale Roffense, John Thorpe 1788 192-4; Faith and Fabric, A History of Rochester Cathedral 1996 206; Handbook to the Cathedrals of England, Southern Division Part II 593-4; The Cathedral Church and Monastery of St.Andrew at Rochester 1900 125; The Cathedral Church of Rochester, Palmer 1899 96-8

2. Encyclopaedia of World Art 1961 "Limoges"

3. For a detailed description see Royal Commission on Historical Monuments, Westminster Abbey

4. John Blair, The Limoges Enamel Tomb of Bishop Walter de Merton, reprinted in Postmaster September 1994, 35

5. Sketch 42n.

6. Registrum Annalium Collegii Mertonensis 1567-1603, ed. J.M. Fletcher 332, 337

7. Sketch 41-2

8. D.A.H. Clegg, quoted in Annual Report of Friends of Rochester Cathedral 1997-8 27-8. See also Palmer op. cit.97 "The effigy is remarkable for the anachronisms it shows"

9. See (i) a MS letter from Dr. Hawkins to Warden Bullock Marsham dated 3.8.1849 (ii) a MS Report by Dr. Hawkins, both in Merton College records

10. See previous note.

11. Typed copy of a memorandum by Dr.Hawkins (Emf 135) held in Rochester Cathedral archives at Rochester Public Library

12. See (i) a note added to the memorandum mentioned in the previous note (ii)Rochester and Gillingham Observer 14.2.1930 "Local Ironwork: Ancient and Modern". Edwin Harris

13. For a more detailed account of the administration of the estate see ERM 54-8

Chapter Eleven - Walter's Wealth

1. Stenton 27. Lady Stenton reckoned a multiplier of 15 - 20 times to convert from 12th. to early 20th. Century. The UK COL/RPI indices add a multiplier of around 60 x to move from 1914 to 2000. Overall therefore around 1000 x.

Chapter Twelve - Walter's Legacy

1. Memorandum of Dr. Hawkins cited in note 8, chapter 10
2. e.g. Royal Commission on Historical Monuments, City of Oxford 78
3. Dr. Hawkins' letter to Warden Bullock Marsham cited in note 9, chapter 10
4. Sketch 50
5. WALTER DE MERTON - OBIT 1277 - A REASSESSMENT "IN MEMORIA AETERNA ERIT JUSTUS. AB AUDITU MALI NON TIMEBIT" by R. Peter Plowden-Wardlaw (himself a banker after WW II): Postmaster October 1991 95
6. See ch.7
7. Ibid.
8. CR 16.8.1257
9. B & M 370
10. PR 18.3.1261
11. See ch.9
12. For a brief overview see Encyclopaedia Britannica "Education".

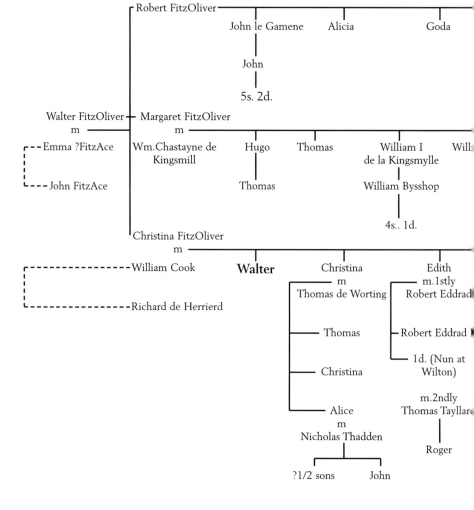

The Family of Walter de Merton

Matilda

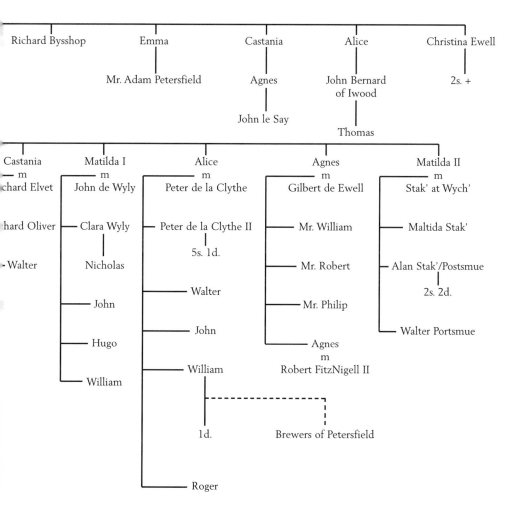

Appendix II

Extract from the Chronicle of Thomas Wykes, Canon of Osney

Eodem anno [anno 1277] in vigilia apostolorum Symonis et Jude, obiit
Walterus de Merton, episcopus Roffensis, de cujus moribus quidam
versificator dixit:-

Presul Walterus Roffensis pontificali
Culmine sincerus, virtute micans speciali,
Qui de Mertona vulgari more vocatus,
Cujus fama bona, gestus super omnia gratus,
Fidus in alloquio, justus, sermone modestus,
Cautus consilio, castus, socialis, honestus.
Dilexit clerum, gratis tribuens alimentum:
Pro quo Walterum benedicit turma studentum.
Oxonie studium per eum quasi plantula vernat,
Conferat auxilium sibi Rex qui cuncta gubernat.

Translation by Thomas Braun, Dean of Merton College.

Walter, prelate of Rochester, his see,
Sincere in rule, of bright integrity,
Called in the common parlance after Merton,
Gracious in all his deeds, of good fame certain,
Faithful and modest, worthy of all trust,
Prudent in council, chaste, good-natured, just,
Loving the clergy, loved by those he fed,
Praised by the troop of students which he led:
Verdant through him are Oxford's studies made.
May the great King of all vouchsafe him aid.

Appendix III

The main part of the inscription placed on Walter's tomb in 1598

Gualtero de Merton, cancellario Angliae sub Henrico tertio, episcopi Roffensi sub Eduardo Primo, re unius, exemplo omnium quotquot extant collegiorum fundatori, maximorum Europae totius ingeniorum foelicissimo parenti, custos et scholares domus scholarium de Merton in universitate Oxon' communibus collegii impensis debitum pietatis monumentum posuere anno Domini 1598, Henrico Savile custode.

Translation by Thomas Braun, Dean of Merton College

To Walter of Merton, chancellor of England under Henry III, bishop of Rochester under Edward I, by the wealth of one man, and by example of all colleges that exist whatever the founder, of the greatest talents of all Europe the happiest parent, the Warden and Scholars of the House of Scholars of Merton in the University of Oxford have at the common expense of the College erected this monument, as loyalty requires, in the year of our Lord 1598, in the wardenship of Henry Savile.

Index

Notes:-

1. Where there are several references, the principal one is in bold type

2. References to pictures/maps are in italic type.